The Gospel in Greasepaint

Creative Biblical Skits for Clowns, Mimes, and Other Fools for Christ

Mark D. Stucky

PICCADILLY BOOKS
COLORADO SPRINGS, COLORADO

Piccadilly Books
P.O. Box 25203
Colorado Springs, CO 80936
USA

International sales and inquires contact:
  EPS
  20 Park Drive
  Romford Essex RM1 4LH, UK
or
  EPS
  P.O. Box 1344
  Studio City, CA 91614, USA

Library of Congress Cataloging-in-Publication Data
Stucky, Mark D., 1956-
    The gospel in greasepaint: creative biblical skits for clowns,
  mimes, and other fools for Christ / by Mark D. Stucky.
        p.   cm.
    Includes bibliographical references and indexes.
    ISBN 0-941599-30-2
    1. Clowns--Religious aspects--Christianity.   2. Drama in
  Christian education.   I. Title.
  BV4235.C47S78 1995
  246'.7--dc20   95-16273

Simultaneously published in Australia, UK, and USA
Printed in the United States of America

ACKNOWLEDGEMENTS

My thanks to Beth Bedsworth for inspiration, suggestions, and collaboration in the creation of "The Lost Sheep" and "A Morning Like This." She also contributed the basic stories of "A Fountain of Oil" and "Follow that Star" which I modified to fit into this collection.

My thanks also to Kirsten Klassen for her many editorial suggestions on my work.

TABLE OF CONTENTS

---

*(Parenthetical numbers represent the minimum number of clowns required to perform the skit.)

IN THE BEGINNING

Face to Face
with Greasepaint

In 1857 Anthony Trollope wrote: "There is, perhaps, no greater hardship at present inflicted on mankind in civilised and free countries than the necessity of listening to sermons."* As someone who has both preached and listened to innumerable sermons, I know that many people would still agree with Trollope. Sermons, like left-over Brussels sprouts, are good for us but often taste stale and lifeless. People hunger for fresh interpretations of the eternal gospel. One such creative translation, which became a movement in the late sixties, is clown ministry.

In 1983 I attended a clown-ministry workshop, and the clown within me was born. When a friend and I started clowning in local religious settings, we found few helpful published skits. All the skits we performed we created ourselves. We wished we could buy a large published collection of skits to use as a resource.

Those wishes and skits were the seeds for *The Gospel in Greasepaint.* The skits are based on selected biblical texts, ranging from the first chapter of Genesis to the last chapter of Revelation. The collection contains seasonal themes ranging from New Year's to Advent, narration varieties from total pantomime to illustrated sermons, and casting from one clown to five or more.

---

*Quoted by Henri J. M. Nouwen, *Creative Ministry* (New York: Image Books, 1978) p. 23.

These skits rely on visual action which can only be partially summarized on these pages. As you read these narrations, you must fully engage your imagination in order to "see" the skit.

The skits were written primarily for silent clowns. A separate Narrator should read slowly, pausing as needed to give the clowns sufficient time to act. Since normal reading speed is too fast, the Narrator must practice with the clowns to get a feel for the right reading pace.

The skits can be adapted for talking clowns, mimes, or "normal" people who want to act out a skit. Feel free to modify the skits as needed. Buying this book gives you the right to act out any skit on an amateur level.

Although for convenience's sake I usually refer to a single clown with the generic "he," with makeup and costume a clown is usually sexless, neither male nor female (as described in Galatians 3:28).

Although I sometimes refer to the skits as occurring in a church sanctuary, the location does not matter. Since some traditionalists may consider a clown in a church sanctuary as heretical, other locations, such as a fellowship hall, may be a better place to introduce the clown ministry concept. Also, the clowns may be accepted more readily if they are felt to be there "for the children," rather than as a drama "for the adults."

No matter what you do (especially if you do nothing), someone will not like it. Many of the very people who find sermons boring may also feel scandalized by anything new and different. Therefore, move sensitively, cautiously, and courageously.

"Hello, I'm a Clown"

In a circus, the ringmaster introduces the acts. I will introduce one act today. I will introduce you to clowns.

Clowns can always be found in a circus. In a circus we can marvel at, but not really identify with high-wire performers or lion tamers. Their skills, daring, and experiences are beyond us. We can, however, easily relate to the clowns. Clowns are the bumblers who identify our own faults and weaknesses. Clowns are the servants, with no apparent power, who put themselves down in order to lift others up.

Clowns as servants can be found at a rodeo. Despite their constant playing around, rodeo clowns serve a critical function. When a cowboy is thrown from a bull, the clowns are responsible for distracting the bull until the cowboy can safely get away. As they imitate the bull and hide in the barrel, the clowns become a kind of "savior," risking their own lives to save the life of a cowboy.

Clowns have not always been just in circuses and rodeos. Prior to the 12th century, the clown symbol was often used in the church community. Clowns provided comic relief, they acted out gospel meanings, they "held up mirrors" for people to see themselves. But when they parodied the abuse of indulgences and other forms of church corruption, they were accused of being satanic, and were eventually cast out of the church. Excommunication and condemnation is an old tool of religious groups. Centuries earlier the Pharisees and chief priests accused Jesus of being satanic and eventually had him killed.

Jesus, who used dramatic symbols and parables to teach people about the kingdom of God, would have loved clowns. Jesus took on human flesh, walked among us, and died on the cross to *show* God's great love for us. In a world saturated with words, clowns *show* rather than tell. Clowns can act out symbols and parables of life, death, and resurrection. Clowns can visually demonstrate what it means to be a Christian. Clowns can dramatize the gospel in greasepaint.

The visual image of a clown's face has religious significance. A white face is a universal symbol of death. Color is a symbol of life. A clown's color applied over white symbolizes life triumphing over death in the resurrection.

Clowns can justify their actions by quoting 1 Corinthians 4:10, "We are fools for Christ," and 2 Corinthians 11:1, "I hope you will put up with a little of my foolishness." Foolishness may not always be what it seems. God's wisdom may not always seem rational or wise to us. 1 Corinthians 1:25 says, "The foolishness of God is wiser than man's wisdom." God's wisdom does not always seem rational or wise to us. Jesus told his followers to do very strange things such as loving your enemies, giving your money away, and dying in order to live. The wisdom of God's apparent foolishness can be dramatized by clowns.

Clowns can serve as symbols for Christian para-doxes. One such paradox is that hope always follows tragedy. In tragedy there is only defeat. In comedy, defeat is followed by victory, the fall is followed by a lifting up. In that sense the gospel is a comedy. Grief and tears are followed by joy and laughter. Death is followed by resurrection. The clown demonstrates resurrection. "The clown is constantly defeated, tricked, and tromped upon. He is infinitely vulnerable, but never finally defeated."* No matter what happens the clown rises and comes back for more.

Clowns help us laugh at sorrow and defeat. Laughter counteracts fear, anger, and depression. Laughter is good medicine for body and soul.

Let us welcome clowns as ministers to our bodies and souls.

---

*Harvey Cox, *The Feast of Fools* (Cambridge: Harvard University Press, 1969) p. 142.

How to Create a Clown

Anyone Can Do It

Do you have doubts about being a clown? You're not sure you're cut out for it?

I was never a likely candidate for clowning. I am inherently shy, reserved, and introverted. I usually dislike being the center of attention. My face generally shows so little emotion that people hardly know what I'm feeling.

Clowning was far from my sense of identity until one fateful summer a friend went to a clown ministry workshop, and . . . somehow . . . I went, too. I was curious. I wanted to know what it was all about. I thought it might be good therapy. I was right. Overcoming a lot of anxiety, I found clowning to be fun.

If I can be a clown, anyone can.

What Supplies Do You Need?

How do you begin clowning? Sources in the bibliography offer far more information than I can present here, but still I feel compelled to give a basic introductory lesson.

Can you guess the best time of year to become a new clown? Halloween is perfect because stores are full of wigs, costumes, makeup, and funny props. Many other people dress strangely on Halloween, so you'll hardly look out of place.

Thrift stores that sell used clothing are invaluable sources of cheap, colorful combinations of outrageous clothing—especially the stuff nobody else wants. Since

13

professionally made clown costumes and accessories are expensive, as a beginner you should experiment with cheap items, at least until you have developed an established character. Cheap stuff may be all that you ever need.

Mimes have an easier wardrobe. Dark clothes (blue or black) and socks (no shoes) are all that's required.

The water-based makeup kits available at Halloween will do for a start, but oil-based makeup works much better (and won't run down your face in hot weather). Oil-based makeup is not expensive, so why not use the best?

Basic clown makeup ingredients include a tin of clown white, black lining pencil, Carmine red lining stick, baby powder, powder puff or sock, mirror, vegetable or baby oil, soft brush, and paper towels. These can be obtained at novelty, costume, or theatrical supply shops. They can also be ordered through the mail, if you live far from clown civilization. Two such sources are Contemporary Drama Service, Box 7710, Colorado Springs, CO 80933 and Clown Ministry Cooperative, Box 24023, Nashville, TN 37202.

Clown Classifications

Clowns are usually grouped into three main types. The Whiteface clown, as the name signifies, has a face completely covered with white greasepaint. The mouth, nose, and/or eyes are highlighted with color. In a group of clowns, the Whiteface is usually the "smart" one and wears the classiest costume.

The Auguste (pronounced ah-GOOST) clown is the exaggerated bumbler. He has white only around the mouth and eyes (thus highlighting the most expressive parts of the face), with color added to the nose and

Auguste

Tramp

Whiteface

cheeks. The Auguste clown wears outrageously unfashionable clothing.

The Tramp clown is the sad, down and out hobo who makes the audience want to lift him up. He looks as if he hasn't shaved for a week, and wears old, torn clothing.

Applying Makup

The first step is to put on the clown-white greasepaint foundation. Dab some clown white on your face and rub it unto appropriate sections of the skin. Use only enough to look white, not grey. You can remove excess or refine designs with a wet towel or cotton swab.

To keep the greasepaint from smearing, the face is coated with a thin layer of baby powder. You can use a puff to do this, but the most efficient and least messy method is to put several handfuls of powder into a sock, tie the sock closed, and pat the sock gently against your face, letting the powder sift through the sock and onto the greasepaint. Brush away any excess powder.

Use a red lining stick to highlight your mouth, nose, and cheeks as desired. However, do not use the Carmine red around the eyes because the pigment is potentially harmful to the eyes, also, red around the eyes makes a clown look angry. The colored lines you draw should follow the natural lines of your face. Look in the mirror and, make different faces at yourself; you will see the lines to follow and highlight. Doing this will make your face more expressive. Powder the colors as you did the white.

Outline features or add any desired black features with a black makeup pencil. Powder again as before.

Use power carefully; too much powder dulls the colors. Brush off any excess powder with a brush and then a damp paper towel. Brush off, but do not rub, lest thou shalt smear thy face.

A tramp clown uses black for whisker areas, brow lines, and crow's feet around the eyes. Some red is used on the nose and cheeks.

Mimes make a white oval, outlined in black, on their faces. The oval extends from just above the eyebrows to the bottom of the chin. A thin black vertical stripe is then made over each eye; each line runs the eyebrow, down over the eyelid, and down the cheek.

Add a red sponge nose, wig, hat, and costume as desired.

To remove makeup, apply vegetable oil or baby oil, and rub off with paper towels. Then wash with soap and water.

Experiment with different faces until you find something which you consistently like, and which fits the character you are developing.

PENTATEUCH

| Genesis
1:1-2:3 | # God Creates a
Beautiful World |

Theme: Creativity, Nature Sunday.

Cast: Narrator, one clown.

Level: Children/adult.

Props: Drum, easel or blackboard, large white/black posterboards, chair, magic markers or paint, and figures of stars, moon, sun, fish, birds, and animals.

The Performance

The stage is set with a large blank, black posterboard set on an easel or blackboard. The lights in this section of the room are turned off. The Narrator slowly reads the creation story from a modern translation of the Bible. At the end of each "day" the Narrator beats a drum.

As the Narrator begins reading, the clown enters and "hovers" beside the black poster.

For Day 1 (1:3-5) the lights are turned on and the clown puts up the white poster beside the black one to represent night and day.

Whenever the Narrator says "God saw that it was good," the clown claps his hands.

For Day 2 (1:6-8) the clown paints clouds and blue water on the white poster.

For Day 3 (1:9-13) the clown paints brown land and green trees.

For Day 4 (1:14-19) the clown tapes a smiling moon and stars on the black poster, and a yellow smiling sun on the white poster. He gets carried away and tapes a few stars on himself.

For Day 5 (1:20-23) the clown tapes figures of fish and birds onto the posters.

For Day 6 (1:24-31) the clown makes balloon animals, or plays with some puppets. He goes out into the congregation, gets one man and one woman to stand up, hugs them, "presents" them to the congregation, and stands back to admire them. He then sweeps his arms over the entire congregation.

For Day 7 (2:1-3) the clown sits in a chair to rest. He blows a kiss to "bless" the seventh day.

The Narrator concludes: "This is the story of God creating our beautiful world. Now we see all that God made, and we know it is very, very good." The clown bows and exits.

Abraham's Big Test

Theme: Suffering, providence, Lent.

Cast: Narrator and two clowns.

Level: Adult.

Props: Bundle of sticks, matches or lighter, altar, rope, toy knife, stuffed animal (sheep or goat), large cross.

The Performance

(The Narrator begins as the clown representing Abraham enters.) **This is a story about Abraham and his big test.**

Abraham and his wife, Sarah, had gotten old (Abraham totters). **But they had no children because Sarah was unable to conceive. This made Abraham sad** (Abraham weeps) **because people in that day thought having no children was a tragedy. What made the situation worse is that God had spoken to him years before about children. God had told Abraham to journey from his homeland** (Abraham walks around) **to the Promised Land, and there God would make Abraham into a great nation.** (Abraham lifts his arms toward the ceiling.) **Abraham was promised many descendants.** (Abraham looks around.) **But God seemingly had forgotten that promise.** (Abraham sinks to floor.)

But one day God again spoke to Abraham. (Abraham rises and cups his hand to his ear.) **God**

---

*Supporting scripture: Hebrews 11:17-19, James 1:2-4.

promised that Sarah would yet have a baby, even though she was old (Abraham acts surprised), and they should name the boy "Isaac."

God kept His promise. ("Isaac" clown enters and runs to Abraham. The clowns embrace and dance together.) And Sarah had a son. Abraham and Sarah named the boy Isaac, which means "laughter," and they all laughed with joy. (Isaac leaves or stands at a distance.)

One day God spoke to Abraham again. (Abraham cups his hand to his ear.) Abraham listened eagerly because God had brought him joyous news before. But this time it was different. God was testing Abraham's faith.

God said, "Abraham, take Isaac, your only son, whom you love, and go to the place called Moriah, which means 'the place where the Lord provides.' Go to the mountain top that I will show you, and sacrifice Isaac as a burned offering to me."

(Abraham is stunned and horrified.) "No!" Abraham thought. "How can this be? How can a good God ask me to do such a monstrous act?"

(Lights dim. Abraham lies down and tosses about.) Abraham got little sleep that night. God had promised him a son in his old age, God had given him that son, and now God demanded to have his son back. (Abraham sits up and buries his face in his hands.) How could God want him to murder his own son? What about the promise of many descendants through Isaac? Abraham did not understand.

(Abraham stands as the lights brighten.) Abraham rose early the next morning. Even though God's command seemed crazy, he would obey. (Isaac walks to Abraham. Abraham embraces him sorrowfully.) He would sacrifice his only son.

(Abraham gathers sticks and gives them to Isaac.) **Abraham cut wood for the offering fire, and when he had enough, they set out for Mount Moriah.** (The clowns walk around in a circle. Abraham holds up a paper heart, tears it in half, and holds the pieces so that Isaac can't see them.) **Abraham's heart was breaking, but he tried to hide his feelings from his son.**

On the third day, Abraham looked up and saw the place provided by the Lord (Abraham points upward, and they mime climbing motions), **and they began climbing the mountain.**

Isaac asked Abraham, "Father, we have wood and fire, but where is the lamb for the offering?" (Isaac mimes the question, holding up the bundle of sticks and lighting a cigarette lighter or match.)

(Abraham cringes.) **Abraham felt as if the knife already plunged into his heart had been twisted, but he answered, "My son, the Lord** (Abraham points up) **will provide the lamb for the burned offering." Abraham thought, however, that his own son was to be the lamb that God provided.**

(The clowns end up beside the church altar.) **When they reached the top, Abraham built an altar out of the stones that he found on the ground. Then he placed the wood on top of the altar.** (Abraham pretends to build the altar, placing the bundle of sticks on the top.) **It was time for the sacrifice.**

(Abraham hugs Isaac farewell, ties him up with a rope, and lays him on the altar. Isaac looks puzzled at first, and then scared.) **Abraham bound Isaac with a rope and laid him on the altar. Abraham took a knife and prepared to kill his son.** (Abraham raises a toy knife.)

But the angel of the Lord called out Abraham's name, "Abraham! Abraham!" (Abraham drops the knife and cups his hand to his ear.) "Do not lay a hand on the boy. Do not do anything to him. Now I know that you love and respect God more than anything else in the world—even more than your only son." (Abraham removes the rope and pulls Isaac off the altar. They embrace and dance.)

Then Abraham noticed a ram caught by its horns in some rocks. (Abraham "finds" a stuffed animal and places it on the altar.) Abraham sacrificed the ram in the place of his son and called the top of the mountain, "The Lord Will Provide." This produced a saying: "On the mountain of the Lord it will be provided."

(The clowns take away the stuffed animal and place a large cross on the altar. The clowns leave. The Narrator steps behind the pulpit or the altar.)

This story in Genesis foreshadows an even more important story in the New Testament. The region of Moriah is the area where Jerusalem later stood and where Jesus was crucified.

Several parallels exist between the stories of Abraham's test and Jesus' crucifixion. Abraham was tested, and so was Jesus. Isaac was Abraham's beloved only son, and Jesus was God's beloved only son. Both sons were to be offered as a sacrifice in the region of Moriah. In Genesis, the ram took the place of the sacrifice and saved one person. In the New Testament, Jesus took the place of the sacrifice, and saved all who would believe in him. Figuratively speaking, Abraham received Isaac back from death. Jesus actually died and came back from death by resurrection.

The story of Abraham and Isaac contains two themes that can hardly be stated more dramatically or emphatically. God tests, but God also provides.

We don't want a god who tests. We want a nice soft god, a god who demands nothing from us. We believe in a loving, gracious god. However, a god who sometimes seems to act like the Devil is hard to fit into our faith.

God tests, but he also provides. God furnishes, supplies, prepares, and cares for us. This, too, is a problem for many people. One commentator* said: "To assert that God *provides* requires a faith as intense as does the conviction that God *tests*. It affirms that God, only God and none other, is the source of life." In a world that hardly believes in God at all, the claim that God alone provides is as much of a scandal as the claim that he tests.

People often live with a paradox. On the one hand, we want a god who only provides, who cares for our needs, but does *not* test. On the other hand, we often do not really believe that God will provide for what we need in our tests.

We don't like the idea of a god who tests. We wish we had only a god who provides. But the Lord our God both tests and provides.

When our faith is tested, we must believe that God provides. We must believe God *did* provide for Abraham. We must believe God *will* provide for each one of us.

---

*Walter Brueggemann, *Genesis* (Atlanta: John Knox Press, 1982), p. 191.

Idols Then and Now

Theme: Idolatry.

Cast: Narrator and three or more clowns.

Level: Children/adult.

Props: A statue, cardboard "10 Commandments tablets," telescope, play money, romance novel, briefcase, television, headphones, toy plane and missile.

The Performance

(The Narrator begins as Clown 1 enters with a statue "idol.") **Long ago, people worshiped idols.** (Clown raises his "idol.") **Idols were objects made of wood, stone, silver, or gold that people considered to be a representation of a god, or even a god itself.** (The clown puts the idol on an altar and bows to it.) **People worshiped these idols by devoting their time and energy to them, considering them to be of supreme value, honoring them, and adoring them.**

(Clown 2 enters with a cardboard "Ten Commandment tablets" and stands near the altar.) **In the Ten Commandments, God condemned idols by saying: "You shall have no other gods but me. You shall not make for yourselves idols or worship them."** (Clown 2 points at his tablets, and then at the idol.) **Only the Lord God, Creator and Redeemer, should be worshiped.** (Clown 2 points up.)

But people did not listen. (Clown 1 puts hands over his ears.) **They made idols. They worshiped them. Their hearts turned away from the true God.**

25

(Clown 1 turns his back on Clown 2.) **Their hearts became corrupt, and they suffered war, bitterness, hatred, disease, and death.** (Clown 1 doubles up and exits holding his stomach.)

As the years passed, people learned more about the universe. (Clown 3 comes in with a telescope.) **They studied astronomy, biology, physics, chemistry. They realized that chunks of rock, or trees, or fashioned images of metal, or the stars, or the planets contained no gods.** (Clown 3 points his telescope at the idol on the altar, laughs at the idol, and puts it away.) **They no longer believed in little gods. But many also forgot the one true God.** (Clown 3 turns his back on Clown 2.)

Since many modern people no longer worshiped God or little gods, they had to consider something else of supreme value. (Clown 3 scratches his head.) **They had to devote their time and energies to something else. So people began to adore other things. They didn't think of it as worship, but in essence it was.** (Clown 3 pulls a large box filled with the following props close to the altar.)

Some people worshiped money. (Clown 3 places bundles of fake money on the altar and bows to it.)

Some people worshiped romance. (Clown 3 kisses a cheap romance novel, places it on the altar, and bows to it.)

Some people worshiped their jobs. (Clown 3 places a briefcase on the altar and bows to it.)

Some people worshiped entertainment. (Clown 3 places a portable television and headphones on the altar and bows to them.)

Some people worshiped alcohol and drugs.

(Clown 3 places a wine bottle on the altar and bows to it.)

Some people worshiped weapon systems. (Clown 3 places representations of bombers and missiles on the altar and bows to them.)

Some people worshiped more than one thing. (Clown 3 plays with various objects on the altar.) **Some people even worshiped these things while** *also* **worshiping the true god.** (Clown 3, while grasping as many things in his hands as possible, bows to Clown 2.)

They didn't think of these things as idols, but they had invented new forms of idols. Some of these new idols were not bad in themselves. In the old days, rocks, wood, and gold were not bad in themselves, either. But people's attitude made the difference. Created things were not meant to be worshiped. They were not meant to be gods. (Clown 3 drops all the items on the altar and leaves.)

We still construct idols. Although the particular things people worship have changed over the centuries, people's characters haven't really changed.

Now I wonder, what things do we idolize?

<table>
<tr><td>Exodus
20:8-11*</td><td># Work, Work, Work</td></tr>
</table>

Theme: Work, recreation, Sabbath, Labor Day.

Cast: Narrator and one clown.

Level: Adult.

Props: Construction worker's hard hat, garbage bag filled with crumpled newspaper, watch or clock, money, Bible, juggling balls, rubber chicken, slices of bread, table, chair.

The Performance

(A clown, wearing a construction worker's hard hat, enters. The clown carries a large plastic garbage bag stuffed with crumpled newspaper and walks hunched over, as if carrying an enormous burden. The Narrator begins.) **I knew a man who worked very hard. He worked, and he worked, and he worked, and he worked.** (The clown walks rapidly in circles.) **He never had time for his family and friends.** (The clown looks at his watch or clock and shakes his head.) **He hardly stopped long enough to eat.** (The clown drops the sack, pulls out a rubber chicken, slaps two slices of bread around it, pretends to take a bite, puts it away, picks up his sack, and continues to walk in circles.) **He went to bed very late** (the clown yawns, drops the sack, and lies on the floor), **and he got up very early** (the clown stretches, rubs his eyes, picks up the sack, and continues to circle). **He got little sleep** (the clown yawns but continues walking) **and was always tired. He worked**

---

*Supporting scripture: Palms 127:2, Eccles. 4:7-8.

like this day after day, week after week, month after month, year after year.

He worked like this so that he would always have enough money. (The clown checks money in his pocket with one hand, without breaking stride.) Even though he always had plenty, he was afraid that his money might run out.

But one day his *strength* ran out. (The clown drops bag.) His exhausted body could take no more work, and he became very sick. (The clown falls face-down on a table.) While he was ill he had plenty of time to read and think. (The clown reads a Bible.) In the Bible, he read about how God created the earth in six days, and rested on the seventh. (The clown counts on his fingers.) He read the Ten Commandments. In the fourth commandment God said: "Observe the Sabbath and keep it holy. You have six days in which to do your work, but the seventh day is a day of rest dedicated to me .... In six days I, the Lord, made the earth, the sky, the seas, and everything in them, but on the seventh day I rested. That is why I, the Lord, blessed the Sabbath and made it holy."*

The man realized he had been working seven days a week, not six. He *never* took a Sabbath rest. (The clown shakes his head sadly.) He never took time to worship God, to be with people, to rest, to re-create, to play. Instead, he had nearly worked himself to death.

Well, he was going to change that! (The clown smiles and nods his head.) When he recovered from

---

*Exod. 20:8-11, *Good News Bible: Today's English Version* (New York: American Bible Society, 1976).

his illness, he went back to work. (The clown gets up and carries the trash bag in a circle but at a slower, more relaxed pace.) **But he did not let himself become so driven, and on the seventh day he stopped.** (The clown drops bag.) **He worshiped God** (the clown bows his head and presses his hands together). **He rested** (the clown sits in a chair), **he spent time with his family and friends** (the clown shakes hands with various people), **and he had fun** (the clown juggles some balls).

He never overworked again. He found that he now felt stronger and healthier (the clown flexes muscles), **he still got almost as much work done as before** (he carries the bag again), **and he enjoyed his work much more.** (The clown smiles and skips out, waving at the people).

With All Your Heart

Theme: Love for God, temptation, sin, Valentine's Day.

Cast: Three clowns.

Level: Children/adult.

Props: Two red balloons with "LOVE FOR GOD" painted on them, a small blue balloon, a large yellow balloon, a large cardboard box with a red heart shape and "MY HEART" painted on the side, a horn, four signs ("TEMPTATION," "SIN," "REPENTANCE AND SELF-DISCIPLINE," "PRAYER AND THE HOLY SPIRIT"), a broom, a crowbar, many small paper hearts.

The Performance

 This skit is mimed with music (such as "Day by Day" from *Godspell*) playing softly in the background. Clown 1 enters with a cardboard box big enough to hold an inflated balloon. A red heart shape and the words "MY HEART" are painted on one or more sides of the box. Clown 1 hugs the box and points at his own chest.

 He discovers an uninflated balloon and inflates it. The balloon bears the message "LOVE FOR GOD," and he joyfully places the balloon inside his box. He happily hugs his box, honking his horn and dancing.

 Two other clowns enter with signs that say "TEMPTATION" and "SIN" hung around their necks. The SIN clown hides behind the TEMPTATION clown. TEMPTATION waves a small blue balloon in a friendly fash-

---

*Supporting scripture: Proverbs 4:23.

ion and gestures to Clown 1 to come nearer. Clown 1 walks toward TEMPTATION, but then glimpses SIN hiding behind TEMPTATION. Clown 1 walks in a circle around TEMPTATION, but SIN, trying to remain hidden, keeps scurrying to the opposite side of TEMP-TATION. Clown 1 stops, looks worried, and begins walking away from them.

TEMPTATION and SIN run around Clown 1 and stop in his path. SIN hides behind TEMPTATION as TEMPTATION now beckons Clown 1 with a large yellow balloon. After some hesitation, Clown 1 finally grasps the yellow balloon. While Clown 1 is distracted by the yellow balloon, SIN sneaks over and grabs the MY HEART box from Clown 1. Clown 1 looks sad.

SIN and TEMPTATION shake each other's hand, celebrating their victory. They take the LOVE FOR GOD balloon out of the box and pop it. Horrified, Clown 1 clutches his chest and begins to cry.

TEMPTATION and SIN laugh at Clown 1, and Clown 1 becomes angry. He tries to grab the box back from them, but the two sneering clowns easily push him away and play "keep-away" with the box.

Clown 1 gets a broom labeled "REPENTANCE AND SELF-DISCIPLINE." With it, he pops the yellow balloon. Now the two other clowns look worried as Clown 1 "sweeps" them with the broom. TEMPTA-TION tumbles over and is chased out of the room by Clown 1. SIN, however, clings tightly to the box while being "swept." Clown 1 is unsuccessful at dislodging SIN with the broom.

Clown 1 then gets a crowbar labeled "PRAYER AND THE HOLY SPIRIT." After a struggle, Clown 1 pries SIN from his box and chases SIN out of the room.

Clown 1 blows up (or returns with) another LOVE FOR GOD balloon and joyfully places it in his box. He celebrates for a moment by dancing.

Clown 1 then pulls out many paper hearts from out of his box and distributes them among the congregation as he leaves.

Helping One Another

Theme: Mutual aid, Brotherhood Sunday.

Cast: Narrator and four or more clowns.

Level: Adult.

Props: Wallet, coat, racing goggles or oversized sunglasses, leather gloves, large hat, portable radio, stuffed animal, fishing line, play money.

The Performance

(A wallet and coat are placed on the floor. Clown 2 freezes in a crouched position. The Narrator begins as Clown 1 enters.) **One day a car owner decided to go for a drive in the country.** (Clown 1 walks toward Clown 2, who is the "car.") **As he walked to his car, he noticed someone's wallet lying open on the sidewalk.** (Clown 2 points at the wallet.) **The cash inside had been stolen. He did not want to get involved with a stolen wallet, so he just walked on.** (Clown 1 steps over the wallet and walks on.) **A little farther on he saw someone's coat on the ground.** (Clown 1 points to the coat, but walks on.) **But he didn't want to get involved with that either, so he just walked on.**

When he got to his car he checked under the hood. (Clown 1 lifts Clown 2's hat or wig.) **He got into the car** (Clown 1 gets on Clown 2's back and puts on racing goggles or sunglasses, and the leather gloves) **and drove off** (Clown 2 carries Clown 1 piggyback). **He had a great time driving.**

---

*Supporting scripture: Luke 6:31, Galatians 6:2.

Soon he saw a car parked beside the road.
(Clowns 3 and 4 enter. Clown 4, wearing a large hat, crouches down very low and freezes.) **The parked car's hood was up** (Clown 3 pulls up Clown 4's hat and looks underneath), **and its battery was dead. The stranded driver was cold** (Clown 3 shivers) **because his coat had been stolen, and he did not have any money to get help** (Clown 3 pulls out his empty pockets) **because his wallet had been in the stolen coat's inside pocket. But the first car owner did not want to get involved, so he just drove on** (Clowns 1 and 2 "drive" past Clowns 3 and 4).

After a while he turned on the radio. (Clown 1 extends the antenna of a portable radio and presses it to his ear.) **He listened to a preacher's sermon based on Deuteronomy 22:1-4.**

"If you see someone's cow or sheep running loose, do not ignore it. (Clown 4 walks along, pulling a stuffed animal attached to fishing line. He turns around, "sees" the animal, and picks it up.) **Take it back to the owner. But if the animal's owner lives far away, or if you don't know who owns it, then take it home with you and care for it.** (Clown 3 wanders around, his hand shading his eyes, looking for the stuffed animal.) **When the animal's owner comes looking for it, give it to him.** (Clown 4 gives Clown 3 the animal, and Clown 3 happily embraces the animal). **Do the same, no matter what someone has lost. If you see someone in trouble, do not ignore him. Help him."** (Clowns 3 and 4 return to their original positions.)

The driver began feeling guilty. He realized that he should have helped the stranded motorist. He saw someone's problem, and therefore, was obligated to help him.

He slammed on his brakes and turned around.
(Clowns 1 and 2 stop and go back to Clowns 3 and 4.)
**When he reached the stalled car, he connected his
jumper cables between the two cars.** (Clown 2 puts his
hand on Clown 4's head, and Clown 4 raises himself
higher.) **The car started!**

Then the first driver showed the second where to
find his stolen coat. (The clowns "drive" over to the
coat. Clown 3 shivers and puts on his coat.) **The man
put on his coat and stopped shivering from the cold.**

Then they found the stolen wallet. The cash was
gone but at least he got his credit cards back.
(Clown 3 picks up the wallet and mimes giving Clown 1
money.) **The wallet's owner was very relieved, and
he wanted to send a reward to the other for helping
him.** But the first man refused (Clown 1 shakes his
head), **saying that he only wanted to do the right
thing.**

With that, both shook hands and drove off.
(Clowns "drive" out.) **Both decided that the next time
they saw someone in need, they were obligated to
help.**

(The Narrator points at the audience.) **The next
time we see someone needing help, will *we* do the
same?**

HISTORY

Walls Fall Down

Theme: Reconciliation, peace, God's power, World Communion Sunday.

Cast: Narrator and three or more clowns.

Level: Children.

Props: Trumpet, cardboard boxes. (The boxes are ordinary boxes painted to look alike on one side. On the opposite side, each has a word such as PRIDE, SELF-ISHNESS, FEAR, HATRED, ENVY, or BITTERNESS painted on it.)

The Performance ━━━━━━━━━━━━━━━━━

(A "wall" made of cardboard boxes is at the front. Clown 1 hides behind the wall as the Narrator begins.)

Do you remember the story of Joshua and the walls of Jericho? (Clown 2 enters, carrying a trumpet.) **The people of Jericho felt safe behind their massive, strong walls.** (Clown 1 peeks over the boxes, waves at the congregation, and pats the wall with a smile. Clown 2 begins marching in circles around the wall and Clown 1.) **They trusted in their walls instead of God.** (Clown 1 sticks his tongue out at Clown 2.)

But God is stronger than any walls. God told Joshua to have his people march around the walls, blow trumpets, and shout. (Clown 2 blows trumpet.) **And God caused the walls to come tumbling down.** (Clown 1 looks surprised, as he suddenly falls through the boxes, scattering them everywhere.)

─────────────────

*Supporting scripture: Ephesians 2:11-22.

That was a long time ago, but we still build walls today. (Both clowns begin picking up the boxes. They build two smaller walls, angled toward each other. Faces of boxes with words printed on them now face the congregation.) **Even you and I build walls. We build our own walls to hide behind, to keep others out, to keep even God out. We build walls made not of brick or concrete but of** (clowns point out the words painted on the boxes and act them out) **pride, selfishness, fear, hatred, envy, bitterness, and many other negative emotions.**

Our walls keep others out, but they also trap us inside. (Clowns try to get out from behind their boxes, but fail.) **After building our walls we don't have the strength to climb over them, or to tear them down.** (Clowns, acting tired, try to remove some of the boxes but can't.)

We need help to tear down our massive, strong walls. That is the reason Jesus came—to break down our walls. (Clown 3 enters. He pulls a box out of Clown 1's wall. Together they remove the boxes until Clown 1 is free. Then Clown 3 dismantles Clown 2's wall of boxes. He shakes hands with Clowns 1 and 2, brings them together in the middle, and gets them to shake hands with each other.)

Jesus came to break down the walls that separate and trap us. He came to tear down the walls separating us from God and from other people. Jesus came to set us free from our walls.

Hearing the Lord Speak

Theme: Bible Sunday, World Day of Prayer.

Cast: Narrator and two clowns.

Level: Children.

Props: Radio, television, Bible, songbook.

The Performance

(Clown 1 enters and stands in the choir loft with a songbook. The Narrator begins.) **This is the story of Sam the choir boy. He lived a long time ago. He lived next to the church and sang in the choir every Sunday.**

(Clown 1 lies down.) **One night after he had gone to bed, he heard a voice say, "Sam, Sam!"** (Clown 1 springs up with his hand cupping his ear.) **The voice was not familiar. Sam thought it must have come from the radio.** (Clown 1 fiddles with a radio.) **He got up to switch off the radio, but it was already turned off. Puzzled, Sam went back to bed.** (Clown 1 scratches his head and lies down again.)

A few minutes later, he again heard the voice say, "Sam, Sam!" This time he thought the voice must have come from the TV. (Clown 1 cups his hand to his ear, gets up, walks to a portable television, and points to the blank screen.) **But he found the TV was already turned off. Again he went to bed.** (Clown 1 shrugs and lies down again.)

A third time he heard the voice say, "Sam, Sam!" This time Sam decided that the pastor next

door must be calling him. Sam ran next door to the parsonage, knocked on the door, and said "Here I am." (Clown 1 runs to a nearby doorway and knocks. A sleepy-looking Clown 2 comes out of the doorway.) The pastor got out of bed and asked Sam what he wanted. Sam told him how three times he heard a voice call his name. The pastor was very wise, and he realized that the voice must be God trying to speak to Sam. The pastor told Sam that the next time he heard the voice he should say, "Speak, Lord, for I am listening." (The clowns return to their "beds.")

Sam went back to bed and when he heard, "Sam, Sam!" He replied, "Speak, Lord for I am listening." (Clown 1 rises and cups his hand to his ear again.) And the Lord spoke to Sam. Sam listened carefully to what God said, and he obeyed God's word. The Lord was with Sam as he grew up, and Sam became a great leader of the people.

Today we also need to hear what the Lord says. (Clown 1 nods.) Even though God usually does not talk with a human voice as he did with Sam, God still speaks to us in other ways. We can hear God's message when we read the Bible (Clown 1 reads a Bible), when we pray (Clown 1 pretends to pray), when we listen to the pastor preach (Clown 1 cups his ear), and when we listen to others who are older and wiser than we are. May we, like Sam, have listening ears.

Returners of the Lost Ark

Theme: Idolatry, discipline, sin.

Cast: Narrator and three or more clowns.

Level: Children/adult.

Props: Cardboard swords and shields, horns, drums, noisemakers, toy arrow-through-the-head, large box painted gold, dowel rods, signs ("GOD," "PROBLEM," "PROBLEM").

The Performance

(The Narrator begins with an empty stage.) **Long, long ago when Samuel was a prophet in Israel, the people's worst enemies were called the Philistines. One day the Israelites went out to fight against the Philistines.** (Several clowns enter from one side. They carry cardboard shields and swords. Marching across the stage, they exit the other side. If only one door is available for entrance/exit, they march in a circle and then exit through the same door.)

The battle was fierce and raged for hours. (Off-stage clowns honk horns, beat drums, blow noisemakers, etc.) **But in the end, the Philistines won.** (Several clowns re-enter, limping and carrying bent shields and swords. One clown might have a toy arrow-through-the-head. They assemble miserably at the front center.) **Many Israelites were wounded or killed. They asked themselves, "Why did the Lord let the Philistines defeat us today?"** (Clowns look at each other and shrug their shoulders.)

Then someone had an idea. (One clown raises his hand and "speaks" to the other clowns, who all shake their heads in agreement.) **He said, "Let's bring God's Ark of the Covenant from its resting place so that it may go with us and save us from our enemies!" Everyone thought that was a great idea, so off they went to get it.** (Clowns leave and return with a large box painted gold or bright yellow. The box is large enough for one person to get inside. Broom handles or wooden dowels are pushed through the sides to serve as handles. Optionally, some plastic angels might be glued to both end tops of the box. "ARK" is carefully painted in large black letters on the side. "MEGAFORCE WEAPON" is scrawled in black letters under "ARK.")

The Ark of the Covenant was like nothing else on earth. It was designed by God! The Ark was built of wood and covered with gold. Inside, the Ark contained the Ten Commandments on stone tablets, a jar of manna that the Israelites had gathered in the wilderness, and Aaron's staff that had produced green buds like a live tree. The Ark represented God's presence among His people.

The people in the army camp were very happy to see that the Ark was with them. (Clowns wave arms and honk horns.) **They thought if the Ark was with them in battle, God would certainly help them win. God would not let any harm come to His Ark!** (Clowns slowly march out with the box, cardboard shields, and swords.)

The Israelites thought they had God in a box. They thought they could make God win the battles for them. They thought the Ark was a Megaforce Weapon. But God would show them they were wrong.

In the distance, the Philistines heard the celebration in the Israelite camp and were afraid. (Several clowns enter, cup their hands to their ears, and tremble.) They said to themselves, "A god has come into their camp. Nothing like this has happened before. We are in trouble!" But the Philistines believed in other gods. (Clowns pray, then march out.) They prayed to their idols, and they became even more determined to be brave since they thought the odds were against them.

Again a terrible battle was fought. (Noise from offstage, as before.) This time the Israelites suffered an even greater defeat. Many Israelites were killed or wounded, and the Philistines captured the Ark. (One clown returns without sword or shield. Limping and weeping, he exits through the other door.) The whole Israelite nation cried over the tragedy of the defeat, and the lost Ark.

Meanwhile, the Philistines victoriously took the captured Ark to a temple of one of their gods, Dagon. (One clown enters and stands rigidly, like a statue. Several other clowns enter, carrying the box and happily honking their horns.) They placed the Ark in the temple beside the idol of Dagon. (They place the box near the "statue" clown. After the other clowns have moved away and turned their backs to the box, the "statue" clown falls down in front of the box.)

The next morning, the people who entered the temple found the statue of Dagon face down on the ground before the Ark of the Lord! (Clowns return, express shock, lift the fallen rigid clown back into position, and walk away.) They raised the idol back up to its original position. ("Dagon" again falls down and spreads his arms.)

The following morning, the people again found that Dagon had fallen face down before the Ark—as if he were worshipping the Ark. But this time the idol's head and hands had broken off in the fall. The idol had been destroyed.

The Lord also sent horrible diseases, with tumors, upon the people of the city that had the Ark. (Clowns shrivel and hide their faces.) The people in the city became afraid of the Ark, and they sent it away to another Philistine city. (Clowns move the box to another spot on the stage.) The same disasters happened there, and the Ark was moved again. (Clowns pick up the box, but can't find a place to set it down.) But no one wanted the Ark, for all the Philistines were afraid of it.

The Philistines knew they could not keep the Ark anywhere in their land. They also could not destroy it, because they were afraid that God would punish them even more. The Philistines decided to return the Ark to the people of Israel. (Clowns leave with the box.)

The people of Israel rejoiced to see the Ark returned. (Several different clowns bring the box back in. Honking horns and waving their arms, they place it in center stage.) But even after all that had happened, many people still did not have the proper attitude toward the Ark. Some of the people, who did not have much respect for God's commands, opened the Ark and looked inside. (Two clowns do this, clutch their hearts, and fall down.) This lack of respect made God angry, and he struck them down. After this tragedy, the people of Israel had proper respect for the Ark and for the Lord.

The Israelites and the Philistines thought they had God in a box. They thought they could own Him and use Him. The Ark was a symbol of God's presence, but it did not contain God.

Today, we have a lot in common with those people of long ago. We like to put God in a box, too. (A clown with the sign "GOD" around his neck is pushed into the box by another clown.) **We want to put God in a box, close the box tightly, and shove the box into some forgotten closet.** (The clown turns his back on the box.) **We feel that we can run our own lives without being bothered by God.** (The clown pulls out a sign "PROBLEM.") **But when we have a problem, we want to be able to go to the box, and have God jump out and help us.** (The clown opens the box, and "God" pops up. "God" takes the sign "PROBLEM," rips it in half, and throws the pieces away.)

But this is not how God operates. (Both clowns shake their heads. God clown leaves.) **If we think God is in a box, all we really have is an empty box.** (The clown goes to the box with another "PROBLEM" sign. Disappointedly, he shows the congregation that the box is empty.) **God is not an almighty asprin or a galactic band-aid who exists only to solve our problems. God is God. God does things God's way. God is involved in our problems, but on God's own terms.**

A God who could fit in a box wouldn't be very much of a God. Let us rejoice that the Lord doesn't fit in boxes.

David's Big Blunder

2 Samuel 11-12*

Theme: Sin, forgiveness, Lent.

Cast: Narrator and four or more clowns.

Level: Adult (very).

Props: Blackboard, blank posterboard, swimsuit poster, crown, sheet of paper, cardboard swords and shields, plate, bottle, envelope, toy arrow, black and white paper dresses, picture of a baby, stuffed animals, cup, black and white paper hearts, chalk, eraser.

The Performance

(A blackboard holds a poster of a woman in a swimsuit. The poster is covered by a blank piece of posterboard. The Narrator begins as the "King David" clown, wearing a paper crown, enters.) **God had chosen and blessed David as king of Israel.** (Clown indicates crown came from above.) **David was a mighty king.** (Clown makes muscles.) **David was a great person, and he loved God.** (Clown bows head and prays.) **But even the greatest of people make mistakes.**

(One or more clowns enter with play swords and shields.) **In those days, kings of various countries often fought wars against each other during the spring, when the land was no longer muddy from the long winter rains.** (David walks around the front, lifting an open palm to the sky as if looking for rain.) **One spring, David sent his chief commander, General Joab, off with his entire army to do battle.** (David

---

*Supporting scripture: Psalms 51.

47

pretends to send the other clowns off. They salute him and march off, exiting.) **They defeated the Ammonite army, and besieged their capitol city. But instead of overseeing the battle, David stayed home in Jerusalem.**

One evening David strolled around his palace roof. From his roof he saw a very beautiful woman taking a bath. (The Narrator removes the blank posterboard, revealing the poster of a woman in a skimpy bathing suit. Alternately, another clown in an outrageous bikini could come in. David leans forward for a better look. His eyes bug out and his jaw drops.) **He sent a messenger to find out who she was. She was Bathsheba, the wife of Uriah the Hittite, one of David's best army officers. David sent for Bathsheba, and they slept together.** (David takes down the poster, embraces it, and exits with it.)

A few weeks later Bathsheba sent David a letter telling him that she was pregnant. (David reenters, pulls a sheet of paper from an envelope, reads it, acts horrified, and begins to pace furiously.) **Oh no! What was he going to do about this scandal?**

Like many politicians before and after him, David decided on a cover-up. He sent for loyal, brave Commander Uriah. (Another clown enters with a toy sword or shield, and bows to David.) **David asked how the battle was going, and Uriah answered all his questions. Then David told Uriah to go home and relax. He was hoping that Uriah would sleep with Bathsheba. Then no one else would know who the real father was.**

(Uriah curls up on a nearby pew.) **But Uriah did not go home. He stayed with the palace servants for the night. When David was told this, he again sum-**

moned Uriah. (Uriah approaches David and bows.)
David asked him why he had not gone home.

**Uriah replied that the Ark of the Covenant and
Israel's army were camped out in hot, dusty, open
fields. If they were suffering hardship, it would be
unfair for him to wine and dine, and to sleep with his
wife.** (Uriah gestures and shakes his head.)

**David's plan had been foiled. David told Uriah to
stay one more day and then go back to the battle.**
(David raises one index finger. Uriah nods.) **David
then invited Uriah for dinner.** (David hands Uriah a
plate and a bottle. Uriah takes a swig.) **David got
Uriah drunk.** (Uriah staggers toward the door, but then
curls up on a pew.) **But even then Uriah did not go
home. Foiled again!**

**David's cover-up was not working. He became
increasingly desperate.** (David paces.) **He had been a
good king, but even good kings can consider themselves above the law.**

(David begins writing on a sheet of paper.) **In the
morning, David wrote a letter to General Joab, saying, "Put Uriah in the front line where the fighting is
the heaviest, then retreat, and let Uriah be killed."
He sealed the letter in an envelope and gave it to
Uriah to carry to Joab.** (David seals the envelope and
gestures to Uriah. Uriah takes the envelope, salutes, and
exits.)

**Uriah innocently gave the letter containing his
own death sentence to General Joab, and General
Joab obeyed David's command. Uriah, along with
several Israeli soldiers, died in the battle.** (Uriah, with
a toy arrow sticking out of him, is carried in by another
clown. The clown places Uriah on the floor. He puts
the "Bathsheba" poster back on the blackboard, but now

a black paper dress covers her body. Then the clown takes Uriah back out.)

Uriah was mourned by Bathsheba, but when the traditional time for mourning was over, David married her. (David takes off the poster's black paper dress, revealing a white paper wedding dress.) **Some months later, Bathsheba gave birth to David's son.** (The Narrator puts up a picture of a baby.)

David's cover-up was complete—but at a terrible price. David was guilty of adultery, conspiracy, endangerment of his troops, and murder. (With each word David sinks lower.) **Any other citizen in the kingdom would be punished by death for such crimes. But no citizen could bring the king to justice because the king was above the nation's law. The king, however, was not above God's law. David thought he had gotten away with his crimes, but God, the supreme judge, knew about them.**

God sent Nathan the Prophet to David. (Nathan enters and walks over to David who is now sitting on a chair. Nathan does not bow.) **Nathan told David a story about a rich man and a poor man.** (Two other clowns enter. The "rich" clown carries several stuffed animals and lots of play money. They "poor" clown carries only one little stuffed sheep.)

"The rich man had great wealth, and many sheep and cattle. The poor man had only one little lamb, but he took care of that lamb as if it were part of his family. (Poor clown hugs his sheep and smiles.) **The lamb grew up with him and his children. The lamb shared the poor man's food, drank from the cup, and even slept in his arms.** (Poor clown pretends to feed the lamb and rock it to sleep.)

One day a visitor came to the rich man's ranch. The rich man did not want to kill one of his own

animals to fix a meal for his guest. (Rich clown looks over his stuffed animals and shakes his head.) **Instead, he stole the poor man's lamb, killed it, and cooked it for the guest's meal.**" (Rich clown grabs the stuffed lamb from the poor clown's arms and places the lamb on a plate. Horrified, the poor clown exits crying. Carrying the platter high, the rich clown also exits.)

The rich man's story caused King David to burn with anger. (David pounds his fists.) **David said, "I swear by the living Lord, the man who did that deserves to die! For having done such a cruel thing, he must pay back four times as much as he took!"**

Then the Prophet Nathan said (Nathan points at David), **"*You* are that man! The Lord God of Israel says, 'You were just a poor farm boy, but I anointed you king over Israel. I delivered you from your enemies. I gave you wealth and power. If this had not been enough, I would have given you even more. Why then have you disobeyed my laws? Why have you done such evil? You had Uriah killed and took his wife. Now as a consequence of your evil deeds, great trouble will plague your family.'"**

(David hangs his head.) **David replied, "I have sinned against the Lord."**

Nathan continued, **"Although God will forgive your sin, your loss of integrity in leadership has already set into motion a chain of tragedies that must run its course."** (Nathan exits.)

David found forgiveness, but his mistake would haunt him the rest of his life. To express his feelings about this humbling experience, David wrote Psalm 51. (The Narrator removes poster of woman. David goes to the blackboard.)

"Have mercy on me, O God (David falls to his knees) **because of your constant love. For I know I**

have broken your law, and my sin is always before me. (David writes "SIN" in big letters on the black-board.) I have sinned against you and done what is evil in your sight. I have been evil from the day I was born; I have always been a sinner.

"What God wants is a humble spirit, a humble and repentant heart. (David holds up a large heart cut out of black paper.)

"God, create in me a clean heart, one filled with clean thoughts and right desires. (The Narrator takes David's outstretched black heart and gives him a white paper heart in its place.)

"Do not cast me away from your presence, or take your Holy Spirit from me. (David shrinks away, but the Narrator takes him by the hand.)

"Wash away all my evil, and forgive me of my sin. (The Narrator erases the chalk letters "SIN.")

"Restore to me the joy of your salvation, and make me willing to obey you." (The Narrator pulls David to his feet and hugs him.)

David made a big blunder, yet God forgave him. Later David and Bathsheba had another son, Solomon. Solomon had children, and those children had children, and out of that line eventually Jesus, the Savior of the world, was born. (The Narrator writes "DAVID," draws a line, and writes "JESUS,") God's amazing grace is shown in his taking some-thing as evil as adultery and murder, and turning it into something good.

If God can forgive David for such evil, he can certainly forgive us of more ordinary sins. To remind us of the power of God's forgiveness, we will receive a "clean heart" today. (All the clowns pass out white paper hearts.)

New Beginnings

Theme: New Year's, transitions, fresh starts.

Cast: Narrator and four or more clowns.

Level: Adult.

Props: Storm sound effects, choir robe or coat, large cardboard boxes, dolls, skull and crossbones sign, bucket, large salt shaker, price tag, cup, wilted flower, fresh flower, cardboard angel wings, leather jackets, mock weapons, teddy bears.

The Performance

(Large cardboard boxes are stacked together to form "Jericho." Dolls are placed on the top box. "Elijah" clown, wearing a choir robe or coat over his shoulders, enters, and "Elisha" clown follows. The Narrator begins.) **This is a story about Elisha the prophet's new beginnings. Elisha (with an "sh") interned as a student prophet under the great Prophet Elijah (with a "j"). Elisha assisted Elijah for many years, until Elijah was old and ready for an unusual retirement. As Elijah and Elisha were walking together near the Jordan River one day, God sent a tornado to pull Elijah directly into heaven.** (Sound effects of a storm are played. Elisha sinks to his knees. Elijah makes flying motions, dropping the robe near Elisha, and exits.)

After Elijah disappeared into the sky, Elisha looked down on the ground and saw Elijah's coat. This particular coat was a symbol of being a prophet. Elisha picked up the coat and put it on (Elisha puts robe on), for he knew that he was Elijah's successor. Elisha had begun his new career as a prophet of God.

From the Jordan River, Elisha walked to Jericho. (Elisha makes exaggerated walking motions.) Do you remember Jericho? Jericho had a violent history. About 500 years before Elisha, during the exodus of the Israelites from Egypt to the Promised Land, Joshua conquered the city. (A third clown enters with a trumpet. He marches around the stack of cardboard boxes, blows the trumpet, and pushes over the boxes. The dolls scatter on the floor.) Its walls collapsed at the blast of the trumpet. All the inhabitants of the city were slaughtered except for the family of Rahab the harlot, because she had helped the Israelite spies. (The third clown holds a sign painted with a skull and crossbones or a "Mr. Yuk" over the boxes, and drops it upon them.) Upon the ruins of the city Joshua placed a curse, saying that whoever would rebuild the city would do so at the cost of his oldest and youngest sons. (The third clown exits, and a fourth clown enters. He stacks the boxes together again, places the dolls on top, "accidentally" knocks two dolls unto the floor, and carries the two dolls off as he cries.) In spite of Joshua's curse, many years later the city was rebuilt. But the sons of the project's foreman both died as a result.

Jericho had a bloody history, but all that was past. Things changed in Elisha's time.

Elisha went to stay with friends in a monastery near Jericho. (Two clowns enter. One puts down a bucket between them.) Some men of Jericho said to Elisha, "Our city is built in a beautiful setting, but our water supply is bad. Our spring is contaminated and causes illness and death. (The clowns hold their bellies.) **Even the crops produce poorly.** (Clown holds up a wilted flower.) **Prophet of God, can you help us?"**

Elisha said, "Bring me a *new* saltshaker filled with salt."

This request puzzled the men (Clowns scratch their heads), **but they did it anyway.** (They give him a large salt shaker, with a large price tag still attached.) **Why did Elisha want salt? Salt in those days was very important. Salt was a seasoning and a preservative. It symbolized all that was valuable, virtuous, and loyal. Elisha wanted a *new* saltshaker because God was doing a new thing in Jericho.**

(Elisha shakes salt into the bucket.) **Elisha poured the salt into the spring and proclaimed, "This is what the Lord says: 'I have healed this water. Never again will it cause death or make the crops fail.'" And from then on the water was excellent to drink and produced abundant crops.** (One clown, using a cup, pretends to take a drink from the bucket. He jumps up and turns cartwheels. The other clown pulls out a beautiful fresh flower.)

Jericho had a new beginning. The place once cursed was now blessed!

After this Elisha left Jericho to travel to the city of Bethel. (Elisha walks around, and the clowns with the bucket exit.)

Like Jericho, Bethel had a famous place in history. It was at Bethel many centuries before Elisha's time, that Jacob dreamed of a heavenly ladder with angels climbing up and down it. (Two clowns with cardboard angel wings enter, swoop around the Narrator, and exit.) **In the dream, God made a covenant with Jacob. When Jacob awoke, he said, "How awesome is**

this place! This is none other than the House of God." Thus, Bethel, which means "House of God," got its name.

Bethel, however, did not remain a godly place. From that wonderful beginning, Bethel slid downhill. King Jeroboam caused the greatest evil and defamed the city's name, a century before Elisha, by setting up an idol of a golden calf. The idol misled people from worshiping the true God. (A clown enters with a sign, painted with a golden crowned cow. He beckons people to follow the gilded cow, and exits.) By Elisha's time the people of Bethel did as they pleased, and they did not like prophets of the Lord.

Walking to Bethel, Elisha hiked uphill twelve miles out of the valley of Jericho and up a mountain ridge. Upon arrival at Bethel, Elisha was exhausted, but the weary traveler got no hospitality. (Elisha is still walking and acts tired.) Instead, an unpleasant surprise awaited Elisha because some of the unsavory people of Bethel heard of his coming. (Two clowns enter, wearing leather jackets, carrying mock weapons, and looking tough.) A teenage street gang came out to meet him. They jeered him and his relationship with Elijah. They might also have beaten, or even killed him, if they had been given the chance.

But Elisha called down a curse on them in the name of the Lord, and two bears charged out of the woods. (Teddy bears on the end of strings attached to the gang clowns "chase" the clowns as they run out the door.) The bears wounded some of the gang members before the gang could escape. Elisha then continued on his way. (Elisha exits.)

Bethel had a new beginning. The place once blessed was now cursed.

The new beginnings of Jericho and Bethel are stories of contrast. The place once cursed was blessed, and the place once blessed was cursed.

Today we can have a new beginning. Many people in the world would like a new start. Some may feel as if their lives have been cursed. They live with seemingly endless discouragement, pain, sorrow, or shame. For such people, this story's message is that of hope. We can find forgiveness, transformation, and resurrection. We can have a new, blessed beginning.

But there is another side of the coin. To some, the story's message is "watch out!" Many churches have people who cause trouble to those around them, and hinder the work of the Lord. Many people are overconfident that God will bless them because they grew up in Christian homes, because they were always "good" people, because they were a Sunday school teacher, or deacon, or pastor. Let us beware of becoming complacent over a record of good deeds in the past.

What happened in the past is over. What happens now is what counts. Today, let us rededicate ourselves to the Lord of new beginnings.

A Fountain of Oil

Theme: Suffering, obedience.

Cast: Narrator and five clowns.

Level: Children/adult.

Props: Tantalus Magic Water Vase, jars, I.O.U, fake money, loaf of bread.

The Performance

("Mother" clown and two "son" clowns enter and huddle together as the Narrator begins.) **There once was a woman with many, many troubles.** (Clown family weeps together.) **Her husband died, leaving her with only her two young sons and a small house. The economy was bad, and she could not find a job. Since welfare did not exist yet, she borrowed money to buy food.** ("Bill collector" clown with fake money stuffed in his pockets dangles a wad of bills in front of the family. Mother writes "I.O.U." on a large piece of paper and gives it to him in exchange for the money. Then the bill collector offers her a loaf of bread for the money. The family starts eating slices of bread as the bill collector exits.)

But the trouble with borrowing money is you have to pay it back, and the woman could not. One day the bill collector came back and demanded his money. (The bill collector returns and shakes the I.O.U. in front of her. The woman shrugs helplessly.) **He said if she could not repay the loan by the next day, he would take her two sons and make them slaves.** (The mother grabs the two sons, and they all tremble. The bill collector exits.) **What could the mother do about this horrible situation?**

She remembered that her husband had followed the prophet Elisha. Elisha was a great man of God. Maybe he could help her. (Elisha enters and walks along opposite the family. The Mother runs to him and kneels before him.) **She found Elisha and told him about the bill collector's threat. She begged him for help.**

Elisha felt sorry for the woman. He went home with her, and told her to bring out anything of value. The family looked through their almost empty house. (The clowns turn out their empty pockets, look around, then show Elisha a bottle. The bottle is a Tantalus Magic Water Vase, an inexpensive magic trick available in a magic shop or catalog. The Vase should be filled with colored water.)

They finally found a small bottle partly filled with olive oil. Olive oil was very important in those days because it was used in cooking, for lamps, and in cosmetics. It was also used in religious ceremonies because it was considered a symbol of joy and plenty.

Elisha told the family to go out to all their neighbors and borrow all the empty jars they could find. The mother wondered what good empty jars could do. (Clowns act puzzled, but then go out and collect bottles planted among the congregation. If this is a children's story, the children can also help.) **Nevertheless, they obeyed Elisha's word and returned with many jars.**

Then Elisha told them to pour oil from their original bottle into a jar until the jar was full, set the jar aside, and then do the same thing with the next jar.

What an odd command. Her bottle was smaller than any of the jars. She would not be able to fill even the first jar, and if she poured all of the bottle's oil into the first jar, there would be nothing left for any of the other jars. But the woman obeyed Elisha's word. (Mother pours water from the Tantalus Vase into the first jar, sets the vase down to let the water out of secret compartment, then repeats with other jars.) She filled the first jar. She filled a second jar, and then another and another until every jar was filled. (Clowns are all amazed.) Only after every jar was filled, did the oil in the original bottle run out.

Then Elisha told them to sell all the bottles of oil. They would be able to pay off their debts and live on the remainder of the money. (The bill collector comes in waving his I.O.U. The Narrator hands the Mother a wad of bills. She pays off the surprised bill collector.) Her two sons were saved from slavery, and they were no longer dirt poor. (Clowns exit.)

Even though she did not understand the reason behind Elisha's commands, the woman obeyed. Her faithful obedience saved her family.

The Spiritual Cycle

Theme: New Year's, transitions, spirituality, renewal.

Cast: Narrator and three clowns.

Level: Adult.

Props: Cardboard boxes, paper chains, ping pong balls or Nerf balls, sign 1 ("LIBERATED, BLESSED, GRATEFUL"), sign 2 ("DISOBEDIENT, REBELLIOUS, SELF-SEEKING"), sign 3 ("DEFEATED, CONQUERED, OPPRESSED"), sign 4 ("REPENTANT, SORROWFUL, HUMBLE").

The Performance

(Several large cardboard boxes sit in a scattered pile. The Narrator begins.) **Imagine for a moment what history would have been like if Hitler had won World War II. Imagine the Nazi army sweeping across all of Europe and into North America in 1944, killing, looting, and destroying. Imagine them taking millions of people transporting them to concentration camps in foreign countries. Imagine that _you_ were put into a slave labor camp, or else grew up in one.**

Imagine that at last Hitler dies, and a more benign dictator takes his place. He releases many people from the camps, and permits them to return home. Imagine that _you_ come back to your parents' and grandparents' homeland. Although the land is still occupied territory, imagine your joy upon returning to a normal life in your own beloved country.

Now you know a little of how people felt in the

time of Nehemiah. (Two clowns, bound with paper chains, shuffle in.) **For 70 years their country had been under foreign occupation, their capital city and temple had been in ruins,** (Narrator gestures to scattered boxes) **and the people had been exiled in a foreign land. But they finally were allowed to return home.** (The Narrator breaks the chains off the wrists of the clowns, and gestures that they are free.) **The temple was rebuilt, and the walls of Jerusalem were repaired.** (The clowns neatly stack the boxes together. Then they lift up their arms and dance.)

Though they were thrilled to be home again, their joy was mixed with sadness. (The clowns bow their heads in sadness.) **The land was still ruled by enemy forces. Jerusalem and the temple were only shadows of their former glory. The spiritual life of the people needed strengthening.**

The whole nation set aside a day to confess their sins. (Clowns kneel.) **Their prayer that day is found in Nehemiah 9:5-37. This is the longest prayer recorded in the Bible, and it retells the entire history of the world up until that day.**

It begins with praise to God ("God" clown enters and pantomimes creating things) **for making the sky, the stars, the earth, and all living creatures.**

It praises God for richly blessing the people of Israel. ("Israel" clown picks up the four signs which are turned so they cannot be read. He stands beside God, who pats Israel on the head, and they both smile. Israel raises sign 1, "LIBERATED, BLESSED, GRATEFUL," so the audience can read it.) **God saved the people from their enemies.** (God puts his arms around Israel in a protective stance.) **God gave Israel land and provided for all of the people's needs.** (God sweeps his arm, showing the "land." Israel starts walking slowly into the "land" with his back toward God, and half-turned away from the audience.)

But the good times did not last. The people stopped listening to God. (Israel covers one ear, and swaggers.) **Instead of obeying God, they began doing terrible things.** (Israel holds up sign 2, "DISOBEDI-ENT, REBELLIOUS, SELF-SEEKING.")

This made God unhappy. (God frowns.) **God decided to stop blessing them. God would let things go wrong for them. God would allow troubles to overcome them.** ("Trouble" clown enters, grabs the posters from Israel, knocks Israel down, stands over him, and holds sign 3, "DEFEATED, CONQUERED, OP-PRESSED.")

The people were unhappy now. They were sorry they had been so bad. They repented of their wrong-doing, they turned from their sin, and they cried out for God's help. (Trouble changes to sign 4, "REPEN-TANT, SORROWFUL, HUMBLE," and looks a little worried. Israel lifts his arms out to God.)

God loved Israel's people very much. When he heard their cries, God forgave them and rescued them. (God throws Nerf balls or ping pong balls at Trouble, who falls over. Israel gets up, holding Sign 1, and walks over to God's side. God pats him on the head.) **God revived and renewed them. Things were good again . . . for a while.**

As soon as things had been going well, the people began to forget God again. (Clowns repeat previous signs and actions.) **Again they stopped obeying God. Again they began doing terrible things. Again God stopped blessing them and allowed troubles to come their way. Again the people were sorry and prayed**

for help. Again God forgave them and helped them. Again things were good . . . for a while.

This spiritual cycle happened over and over again through history, century after century. (Israel runs around the circle, rapidly changing signs.) Even after all this time, the cycle continues today.

(Clowns hold up all four signs simultaneously and freeze.) Can you see yourself in this cycle? Does everything seem to be going well for you? Have you drifted away from God? Have you fallen under a load of troubles? Have you been crying out to God?

You are invited to confess your sins and call for help. God is ready to revive and renew you, time after time.

WISDOM

Job's Sob Story

Theme: Suffering.

Cast: Narrator and three or more clowns.

Level: Adult.

Props: Slide projector/screen, slides of natural phenomena, globe, table, stuffed animals and dolls, bandages, robe.

The Performance

(The Narrator stands between a large globe of the earth and a projection screen. The slide projector is placed in an unobtrusive location. The sanctuary is darkened except for the lights in front which also can be easily turned off. A half dozen dolls and stuffed animals sit on a table in front of—but not blocking—the screen. The Narrator begins.)

Suffering strikes all of us at one time or another. The example of Job can give us strength in our own suffering. The example of Job's friends can teach us what to do and what not to do for our friends who are in anguish. Listen now to the sad story of Job.

Long, long ago, far, far away in a land called Uz, there lived a man named Job. ("Job" clown enters wearing a beautiful bathrobe. He stands beside the table.) **Job was a good and faithful man, who worshiped God** (Job mimes prayer) **and was careful to do nothing wrong. He had seven sons and three daughters, thousands of sheep, camels, cattle, and donkeys, and a large number of hired hands.** (Job lifts up and shows the congregation each doll and stuffed animal.) **He was the richest man in the land. He constantly prayed for each one of his children.** (Job gets on his knees and freezes in an attitude of prayer.) **He was a man who loved God, and was loved by God.**

One day in heaven, the angels came to present themselves before the Lord. Satan, whose name means "Adversary," came with them. ("Satan" clown, dressed in red, enters and walks up to the Narrator.) **The Lord said to Satan, "Where have you come from?"**

Satan answered the Lord (he points at the globe and mimes walking), **"From roaming over the earth and walking back and forth on it."**

The Lord asked, "Did you notice my servant Job? (The Narrator points at Job.) **There is no one on earth as faithful and good as he is. He worships me and is careful to do nothing wrong."**

Satan sneered, "Would Job worship you if he got nothing out if it? You have always protected him, his family, and all that he owns. You bless everything he does. Look how rich he is. (Satan points to the items on the table.) **His livestock could fill the land. But test him. If you took away everything he has, he will certainly hate you and curse you to your face!"** (Satan shakes his fist at the Narrator.)

The Lord replied to Satan, "Very well, everything he has is in your hands, but on Job himself do not lay a finger. (The Narrator extends his hand, points at Job, and then raises an index finger.)

Then Satan left the presence of the Lord. (Satan turns his back on the Narrator and walks over to Job. He circles Job, rubbing his hands and grinning wickedly. He picks up a doll and a stuffed animal from the table, holds them high in the air, and throws them on the floor. Job watches in horror.) **Poor Job! Suddenly disaster after disaster happened. Enemies killed Job's hired men and stole all his cattle, donkeys, and camels.** (Satan sweeps the rest of the stuffed animals off the table.) **Lightning during a thunderstorm killed all his sheep.** (Satan picks up the rest of the dolls, throws them down, and pretends to stomp them with his foot.) **A tornado struck the house his sons and daughters were in, and the house collapsed, killing all inside.**

After all these tragedies, **Job tore his robe in grief** (Job throws off his bathrobe), **threw himself on the ground** (Job gets down on his hands and knees), **and worshiped God, saying, "I was born with nothing** (Job lifts up one empty hand), **and I will die with nothing** (he lifts up the other empty hand). **The Lord gave** (he holds out a doll in front him with his arm extended), **and now the Lord has taken away** (he snatches back his hand and drops the doll.) **May his name still be praised!"** (Job lifts his hands toward the ceiling in praise.) **In spite of everything that had happened, Job did not sin by blaming God for wrongdoing.** (Satan frowns and walks to one side.)

Another day came for the angels to present themselves before the Lord, and Satan also came with them. (Satan returns before the Narrator.) **The Lord again asked Satan, "Where have you come from?"**

Satan answered the Lord, "From roaming over the earth and walking back and forth on it." (Satan gestures as before.)

The Lord asked, "Surely you noticed my servant Job. (The Narrator points toward Job.) **There is no one on earth as faithful and good as he is. He worships me and is careful to do nothing wrong. And he is still**

as faithful as ever, even though you persuaded me to attack him for no reason at all." Satan replied, "Let me touch his skin! (Satan touches the back of his hand.) A man will give up everything in order to stay alive. If he feels physical pain and loss, he will hate you and curse you to your face!" (Satan shakes his fist at the Narrator.) So the Lord said to Satan, "All right, he is in your power, but you must not kill him."

(Again Satan turns his back on the Narrator, circles Job, and grins wickedly.) So Satan left the Lord's presence and made painful sores break out all over Job's body. (Satan dramatically touches Job. Job falls flat on the ground and moans.) Job felt so miserable that he bandaged himself and sat by the garbage dump. (Job goes to the other end of the table and puts on some bandages.)

(Another clown enters and walks over to Job.) Job's wife said to him, "After God has done all these terrible things to you, why are you still trying to be as faithful as ever? Why don't you curse God and kill yourself? Then you would be out of your misery." Job answered, "You are talking nonsense! When God sends us something good, we welcome it. How can we complain when he sends us trouble?" (The "wife" leaves.) In all his suffering, Job still said nothing wrong about God.

(Several clowns enter, walking in the direction of Job.) Several of Job's friends heard about his suffering and decided to go and comfort him. (The clowns stop and stare at Job in amazement.) When they saw Job, they were stunned. They hardly recognized him because of all the sores covering his body. (Clowns begin to cry.) They began to cry and tear their own clothes in their grief for their friend Job. (The other clowns sit on the floor near Job.) Then they sat on the ground with him for a very long time, without saying anything, because they saw that his suffering was too great for words.

At first, his friends helped comfort Job. By being with him, they showed they cared. (Job nods and gives a weak smile.) But after a while they made his suffering even worse. They tried to explain the reasons for his suffering, even though his suffering was impossible to explain. (Job sinks down even lower as the other clowns begin to pompously gesticulate.)

Job's friends self-righteously thought they knew everything about God's ways. They claimed that since sin always produces suffering, suffering proved someone sinned. They claimed God punished evil people and protected good people. Therefore, Job must have done something wrong. (The other clowns all shake their fingers at Job.)

But Job said they were mistaken. (Job looks up and shakes his head.) The real world disproved his friend's theories and pat answers. The wicked often prospered while the righteous suffered. There was no certain cause and effect between sin and suffering.

Job further denied doing anything so bad as to deserve such punishment. Sure, he had not been perfect—but no one could be perfect compared to the Almighty, Holy God. He had not been perfect, but Job had been as good or better than anyone else. Job's suffering and his friend's accusations were unfair.

During the hours Job argued with his accusing friends, Job had moments of weakness, doubts, and bitterness. But he remained essentially righteous—

more righteous than his friends who were not suffering. Job wished that he could speak directly with God, and ask God why all this had happened to him. (Job looks up.)

And finally God did appear to Job . . . .

(The lights go out, and the slide projector is turned on. The Narrator reads excerpts from a modern translation of Job chapters 38-41. While he reads, slides illustrating the verses are shown on the screen. Which passages are read depends on the slides that can be obtained. Slides of the following would be good: thunderstorms, paintings of the creation of the earth or a photograph of the earth from space, stars, clouds, ocean waves, sunrises, mountains, underwater scenes, glaciers, snow, lightning, rain, lions, ravens, mountain goats, bears, donkeys, wild oxen or steers, ostriches, horses, hawks, eagles, works of art depicting God, hippopotamuses, and crocodiles. At the end of the reading and slide show the lights go on, and Job stands up.)

Job responded to God, "I spoke of things I did not understand, things too wonderful for me to know. My ears (Job cups his hand to his ear) had heard of you, but my eyes have seen you (he points to his eyes). Therefore, I despise myself and repent in dust and ashes." (Job crouches down again.)

Then the Lord said to Job's friends (the Narrator points to the other clowns), "I do not like what you have done. (The clowns act stunned and horrified.) You have not comforted my servant Job and have not spoken correctly about me as Job has. Apologize to him, and repent for your simplistic theology. Then Job will pray for you, and I will accept his prayer." (Job's friends shake hands with Job while miming apologies and then leave.)

The Lord never answered Job's questions about why he had suffered. Yet, after his encounter with the Lord, Job did not complain about unanswered questions. The presence of the Lord was far more effective than any logical, rational explanations.

And later the Lord blessed Job and made him prosperous again. (The Narrator walks over to the table, picks up each doll and animal, and hands them to Job. Job hugs each one and places it on the table. Then the Narrator pulls a few more from a hidden box, and also hands them to Job.) The Lord gave him twice as much as before. Many relatives came to comfort Job for his troubles, and each brought a gift. Job had seven more sons and three daughters, and his daughters were the most beautiful in the land. He had herds of livestock twice as large as before. He lived until he saw his great-grandchildren. When he died, he had lived a long and prosperous life.

Happy are the Good Guys

Theme: Good vs. evil, education.

Cast: Narrator and two or more clowns.

Level: Children/adult.

Props: Black and white cowboy hats, black construction paper "footprints," large Bible, apples, fan.

The Performance

(The Narrator begins.) **In the old westerns, the bad guys always wore black hats.** ("Bad" clown, wearing a black cowboy hat, enters and leaves black construction paper footprints.) **They were always villainous, mean, and rotten.** (Bad clown grimaces.) **The good guys always wore white hats.** ("Good" clown, wearing a white cowboy hat, follows and discovers the black footprints.) **They were heroic, kind, and virtuous.** (Good clown smiles.) **A similar contrast between good and evil is described in Psalm 1.**

Psalm 1 says happy are the good guys who do not listen to the advice of the bad guys. (Bad clown puts his hand to his mouth, pretending to shout advice across to Good clown. Good clown cups his hand to his ear for a few seconds, but then shakes his head and covers both his ears with his hands.)

Happy are those who do not follow in the footsteps of the bad guys and act like them. (Good clown begins following Bad clown's path, picking up the paper footsteps, but then he stops, throws them on the ground, and returns to where he began.)

Happy are those who do not join the bad guys making fun of God and people's faith. (Bad clown jeers at some religious symbol like a Bible, a cross, or communion table. Good clown turns his back on him.) **Instead, good guys enjoy obeying God's word, and they study it as much as they can.** (Good clown shows the congregation a large Bible and begins reading it.)

Good guys are like trees, planted by streams, that bear much delicious fruit. (Good clown pretends to be a tree by extending his arms and holding two apples. A third clown enters, picks an apple from one of his hands, and pretends to eat it. If only two clowns are available, the Narrator could substitute for the third clown.) **They succeed in everything they do.** (Good clown and the third clown shake hands.)

But bad guys are not like this at all. They are like the straw that the wind blows away. (Good clown again pretends to be a tree. The third clown points a fan at Good clown, but he stays rooted. Then the third clown points the fan at Bad clown. Bad clown tumbles out the door as if blown by the wind.) **Bad guys will be condemned by God and kept apart from God's people. Bad guys are on the way to their doom, but good guys are guided and protected by the Lord.**

Confession is Good for the Soul

Theme: Confession, Lent.

Cast: Narrator and two clowns.

Level: children/adult.

Props: sign "FUN"/"SIN," chalkboard, long piece of yarn, horn.

The Performance

(A chalkboard holds a sign with the words "FUN" on the front and "SIN" on the back. Clown 1 enters and walks over to the board as the Narrator begins.) **This is a story of the effects of sin. Sin is doing the wrong thing, doing something that hurts yourself and others. Sin often looks attractive. It seems easy, fun, exciting.** (Clown 1 turns over sign to reveal "SIN".) **But there is a price to pay.** (Clown 1 examines both sides of the sign closely, looks furtively around. Then he grabs the sign and runs a little distance away.) **People often ignore the price until it's too late. Among the many people who found this lesson out the hard way was King David. After he had sinned and suffered the consequences, David, in Psalm 32, wrote about his feelings:**

When I did not confess my sin, I felt terrible. (Clown 1 vainly attempts to hide the sign behind his back or under his coat. He looks guilty and sad.) **I became worn out crying all the time.** (Clown cries.) **Day and night, God, it seemed you punished me.** (Clown 2 enters and pushes Clown 1 around.) **I felt**

weak like on a hot, humid summer day. (Clown 1 sinks to the floor.)

Then I confessed my sin to you. I no longer concealed my wrongdoings. (Clown 1 gets on his knees and stretches out the sign to Clown 2.) **You forgave all my sins.** (Clown 2 takes the sign, examines it, tears it in half, throws the two pieces away, and lifts Clown 1 to his feet.) **I sing of your salvation, Lord."** (Clown 1 pretends to sing and dance in celebration.)

The Lord says, "I will teach you the right way to go." (Clown 2 writes "RIGHT WAY" or draws a pointing hand on the chalkboard.) **"I will instruct you and watch over you."**

Seek understanding so things will go well for you. Don't be stupid like a mule that must be controlled with a bit and bridle. (Clown 1 squats on all fours, puts a piece of brightly colored yarn in his mouth, and acts like a very frisky horse. Clown 2, holding the other end of the yarn, pulls on the yarn until Clown 1 settles down.)

People who stubbornly disobey God have many problems, but the Lord helps those who love Him. (Clown 2 pats Clown 1 on the back after he stands back up.) **All who love God, obey Him and shout for joy!** (Clowns hug. Clown 2 motions Clown 1 to follow him. Clown 1 honks his horn and gladly follows Clown 2 as they exit.)

Coming Home

Theme: Suffering, joy, freedom, salvation.

Cast: Narrator and two or more clowns.

Level: Children/adult.

Props: Paper chains, rope whip, drinking glass, sunglasses, paper palm tree, two boxes marked "SEEDS" and "CROPS," paper tears, paper musical notes marked "JOY."

The Performance

(One or more clowns, wearing paper chains around their wrists, enter. They plod along, bent over by the heavy "chains." The "captor" clown follows with a whip made of rope or streamers. The Narrator begins.) **Long ago the people of Israel were defeated, captured, and imprisoned in a foreign land.** (Captor clown whips the other clowns and pushes them down. The captive clowns huddle together miserably.) **They were enslaved in a strange land for 70 years. But one day God caused their captors to set the Israeli people free.** (Captor clown throws away his whip, lifts each clown up, breaks the chains, and gestures for them to leave.) **Coming home again, their song of joy was written down as Psalm 126.**

When the Lord brought back the captives to Jerusalem, we were like people who dreamed—and found our dreams came true. (Clowns rub their eyes and touch things to make sure they are real.)

Our mouths were filled with laughter, our

77

tongues with songs of joy. (Clowns laugh and dance together.)

Then it was said among the other nations, "The Lord has done great things for them." (Captor clown at one side points at the ceiling and then at them.)

The Lord *has* done great things for us, and we are filled with joy. (Clowns joyfully point toward the ceiling, then to themselves.)

Lord, may all our fortunes be restored as cool water refreshes a desert land. (One clown puts on a huge pair of sunglasses, holds a paper palm tree, and pretends to sip from a drinking glass.)

People who sow in tears, will reap with songs of joy. Those who cried as they sowed their seeds, will return with abundant crops of joy! (A sad clown carries a box marked "SEEDS." He takes out paper teardrops and scatters them about. Then he picks up a second box marked "CROPS" from which he pulls out paper musical notes marked "JOY." The clowns distribute the "JOY" notes among the congregation as they exit.)

Some Wisdom a Day
Keeps the Devil Away

Proverbs
3:13-15*

Theme: Education, graduation, back to school.

Cast: Narrator and two or more clowns.

Level: Children/adult.

Props: Graduation mortarboard, Bible, signs ("WIS-DOM/LIFE," "WISDOM/HOPE"), large cardboard box, scrub brush, sticks, soft object like a feather or pillow, slice of bread, box of Twinkies, apple, Coke can, paper hearts, yellow happy face, saltshaker, coat, bundle of money on a string.

The Performance ▬▬▬▬▬▬▬▬▬▬

(The Narrator begins.) **The book of Proverbs is devoted to wisdom. Its theme is "some wisdom a day keeps the Devil away." Here are some of its words of wisdom.** (Clown 1 enters.)

Listen! Wisdom is calling out. Reason is making herself heard. "I appeal to you, people. I call to everyone on earth. Listen to my excellent words. All I tell you is right." (Clown 1 cups his hand to his ear and listens.)

"I love those who love me, and those who seek me find me. The respect for the Lord is the foundation of wisdom, and knowledge of the Holy One is understanding." (Clown 1 looks up to the ceiling and then bows low. He pretends to look for something with his hand shading his eyes. On top of a Bible he finds a

---

*Supporting scripture: Proverbs 4:7; 8:1, 4, 6, 17, 34-35; 9:10; 15:1, 16-17; 16:18; 17:22; 19:2; 23:5, 24:14; 25:20, 21-22, 28.

79

graduation mortarboard and puts it on. He holds up a small sign "WISDOM.")

Wisdom tastes sweet to the soul. If you find wisdom, you will have hope. (Clown 1 pretends to take a bite out of the sign and pats his tummy. He turns the "WISDOM" sign over, and it says "HOPE.")

Blessed is the one who finds wisdom, the one who gains understanding, for wisdom is more profitable than silver and yields better returns than gold. She is more precious than diamonds and rubies. Nothing you desire can compare with her. Wisdom is supreme. Therefore, get wisdom, Even if you must sacrifice all you have, get understanding. (Clown 2 enters with a handful of fake money and an imitation diamond necklace. He tries to buy the WISDOM sign with the money and then the necklace, but Clown 1 refuses to part with it.)

Here are some assorted sayings by wisdom about how to live a better life.

A harsh word stirs up anger, but a gentle answer turns away wrath. (The two clowns face each other and pretend to argue. They wave hammers or sticks at each other. Then Clown 1 stops and gently offers the other clown something soft, like a feather, marshmallow, sponge, or pillow. Clown 2 accepts it, and they hug each other.)

Only a little, but with reverence for God, is better than great treasure and great trouble because of it. Better to eat only a slice of bread with someone you love than to eat expensive desserts with someone you hate. (Clown 1 prays and then happily eats a slice of bread. Clown 2 has a large box of Twinkies, but he only clutches them possessively and looks around suspiciously.)

Don't try to get rich because wealth can disappear as if it sprouted wings and flew away. (Clown 1 pulls a bundle of play money on a long string. Clown 2 tries grabs the money, but the bundle is pulled out of his grasp.)

Pride leads to destruction, and arrogance will make you fall. (Clown 2 walks around with his nose in the air, his thumbs hooked in his lapels, looking as proud and arrogant as possible. With his nose in the air, he doesn't notice some object on the floor. He trips over it, sprawling into a heap.)

Enthusiasm without wisdom can cause trouble. A person without self-control is like a house with a wall that has fallen down. (Clown 2 jumps around, waving his arms, dancing crazily, and runs into a large box with windows and a door painted on it. He knocks the box over, revealing Clown 1 with a scrub brush, pretending to take a shower. Embarrassed, Clown 1 tries to cover up.)

A broken heart makes you sick, but a cheerful heart is a good medicine. (Clown 2 clutches a torn paper heart to his chest and holds his stomach. Then he tapes a yellow happy face to the two pieces of the heart, mending them together. He happily dances off.)

But being happy-go-lucky around a person whose heart is breaking is as bad as rubbing salt in his wounds or stealing his coat in winter. (Clown 1 slowly and sadly tears a large red paper heart in half. Clown 2 dances around him, poking him in fun, and wearing a huge silly grin. Clown 2 sprinkles salt from a saltshaker unto the torn paper heart. Clown 1 pretends to be in great pain. Clown 2 takes Clown 1's coat, and Clown 1 shivers.)

If your enemy is hungry, give him food! If he is

thirsty, give him something to drink! This will make him feel ashamed of his behavior, and God will reward you. (After taking Clown 1's coat, Clown 2 hits him with a stick, knocking him down. Clown 2 walks away, and then rubs his stomach. He searches his pockets for something to eat, but finds only an empty candy bar wrapper. Clown 1 gets up, walks over to Clown 2, and offers him an apple and a Coke. Clown 2 is thunderstruck. He accepts the apple and Coke, begins crying, and hugs Clown 1.)

Blessed is the one who listens to wisdom, for whoever finds wisdom finds life and receives blessings from the Lord. (Clown 1 turns a "WISDOM" sign over and it says "LIFE.")

PROPHETS

Isaiah's Christmas Greetings

Theme: Advent, Christmas.

Cast: Narrator and one clown.

Level: Adult.

Props: Large sunglasses, manger, doll, banner ("IMMANUEL, WONDERFUL COUNSELOR, MIGHTY GOD, EVERLASTING FATHER, PRINCE OF PEACE"), crown, throne.

The Performance

(The doll and manger are at center stage. All other props are hidden behind the manger. The Narrator begins.) **Did you know that a Christmas card can be found in the Old Testament? Long ago the prophet Isaiah looked into the future and foresaw the birth of Jesus. In 7:14 and 9:2-7 Isaiah gives this Christmas greeting.**

(Lights are switched off until the room is darkened, but still illuminated enough for people to see the action. The melody of "O Come, O Come Emmanuel" is played. A clown, wearing large sunglasses, gropes down an aisle, occasionally bumping into a chair or pew. As the music ends he reaches the front and a spotlight illuminates the manger. The clown removes his sunglasses. Squinting, blinking, and rubbing his eyes, he walks cautiously toward the manger.) **The people walking in darkness have seen a great light; on those living in the land of deep darkness a light has shined.**

84

(The clown's caution changes into delight as he finds the baby doll wrapped in white cloth in the manger. Lifting up the baby for the people to see, the clown also unfurls a banner which says, "IMMANUEL, WONDERFUL COUNSELOR, MIGHTY GOD, EVERLASTING FATHER, PRINCE OF PEACE.") **For behold, a virgin has conceived and given birth to a son, and has called Him Immanuel, which means "God with us."** (Holding the baby in one arm, the clown points to the first name, Immanuel, on the list.)

For to us a child is born, to us a son is given (the clown hugs the doll, miming "to us") **and he will be our ruler** (the clown places a tiny crown on the doll's head).

And he will be called Wonderful Counselor (the clown points to each name in turn on the banner), **Mighty God, Everlasting Father, Prince of Peace.**

(The clown "sits" the doll in a small chair decorated like a throne. The tall headrest has "POWER" and "PEACE" written on it.) **His royal power will grow without end. He will reign on David's throne and over his kingdom, establishing and upholding it with justice and righteousness from this time on and forever!** (The clown lifts the throne and doll into the air, and exits down the center aisle. As he leaves the lights are turned back on in sequence to "follow" his movement. The congregation then sings "O Come, O Come Emmanuel" and/or "The People That in Darkness Sat.")

The Divine Diner

Theme: Salvation.

Cast: Narrator and three clowns.

Level: Adult.

Props: Table, signs ("DIVINE DINER," "MENU"/ "SALVATION," "GOD LOVES YOU"), clock, play money, watering can, trick flower or drawings, bag of potato chips.

The Performance ▬▬▬▬▬▬▬▬▬▬▬▬▬▬

(A large sign "DIVINE DINER" stands behind a table with a clock sitting on it. The Narrator begins as the clowns enter. Clown 3, the "God" clown, stands by the sign.) **Are you hungry? Are you thirsty?** (Clowns 1 and 2 hold their stomachs and throats, then nod.) **All who are hungry and thirsty are invited to God's diner. Here is the invitation.** (God clown points at the sign and beckons to Clowns 1 and 2. Clown 1 checks his empty pockets.)

Don't worry about paying for the meal. At my divine diner you can buy and eat without money. (Clown 1 is very surprised. He walks over to the table. God clown hands him a large folded posterboard. The outside says "MENU." Clown 1 opens it up, and the inside says "SALVATION." Clown 1 smiles and beckons to Clown 2 to join him.)

(Clown 2, however, walks away from the table, pulls some money out, lays it on a chair and opens a bag of potato chips.) **Why spend money on things that** don't really satisfy your needs? **Why buy junk food when your soul is hungry?**

(Clown 2 turns his back on the others and continues to eat potato chips.) **Seek me while there is time.** (God clown points to the clock.) **Repent, turn around, stop rejecting me, and I will forgive you and save you.**

(Clown 1 has continued beckoning to Clown 2. Clown 1 finally stops and scratches his head.) **Even when things seem senseless and hopeless, remember that my ways are not your ways, that my thoughts are higher than your thoughts.** (Clown 1 and God clown use their hands to show different heights.)

The rain and snow do not evaporate back into the air until they have watered the seeds in the ground, making them sprout and grow and produce more seed. (God clown pretends to water a trick flower or a poster of a drooping flower, then he brings the flower to life.

My word that I speak also does not return to me until it finishes the job and achieves my desire. (Clown 2 discovers a piece of paper in his potato chip bag. He unfolds it. Astonished, he shows the people that it says: "GOD LOVES YOU." He throws the potato chip bag away, and walks to the diner. God clown gives him the SALVATION menu.)

When my word accomplishes my purpose, you will live in joy and peace, and the whole creation will celebrate with you. (The clowns all hug and dance out.)

God's Grim Graffiti

Theme: Pride, judgment.

Cast: Narrator and three or more clowns.

Level: Adult.

Props: Table, blank posterboard, sign (see text), sign holder, chairs, plastic or paper cups (some painted gold), crown, noisemakers and party gimmicks, yardstick.

The Performance

(A table with several chairs and a bulletin board or blackboard are in front of the congregation. The table and board are angled so that the clowns and the congregation will be able to see the board. The table has a number of paper cups set on it. The Narrator stands behind the bulletin board so that the people cannot readily see him. Several clowns enter. One, "King Belshazzar," is wearing an aluminum foil crown. The clowns stagger over to the table, sit down, and begin making party noises with horns and noisemakers. The Narrator begins.)

King Belshazzar really knew how to throw a party. At a single party he entertained a thousand guests. The wine flowed freely, and everyone had a great time. The people could afford to enjoy themselves, they thought, because Babylon was the greatest, most powerful nation on earth. Their gods, also, were unequaled in the heavens.

Drunk with both wine and power, King Belshazzar became dissatisfied with his rather ordi-

nary wine goblets. (King holds up a cheap cup.) **He remembered the elegant gold and silver goblets taken from the Israelite temple 70 years before.** He ordered those goblets to be brought and used at the party. (Another clown passes out gold spray-painted cups. Clowns pretend to drink from them.) **From the holy Israelite vessels everyone began drinking wine, and as they drank, they praised their idols made of stone, wood, bronze, silver, and gold.**

(The Narrator puts his hand over the poster so that all can see his hand—but only his hand. He moves his hand as if he were writing. All the clowns see the hand, drop their cups and noisemakers, and huddle together in fear.) **Suddenly the party stopped. A large hand— just a disembodied hand—was writing strange words on the palace wall.** (The Narrator's hand flips the posterboard around to reveal the words printed:

N	N	W	D
U	U	E	I
M	M	I	V
B	B	G	I
E	E	H	D
R	R	E	E
E	E	D	D
D	D		

The King shakes all over and bites his fingernails.)

Everyone was panic-stricken. Nothing like this had ever happened before. What did the strange words mean?

The king called for his magicians, astrologers, priests, and philosophers to tell him the meaning of the ghostly words. He declared that he would richly

reward whomever could give him the translation. (The king gestures at the other clowns, but they just look at each other, scratch their heads, and shrug their shoulders.) **But no one could understand the message.**

Then someone told the king about Daniel, a very wise Israelite, who had revealed great mysteries to others. ("Daniel," using a yardstick as if it were a cane, enters, and the King gestures to him.) **So the king called Daniel and told him, "Daniel, I have heard that the spirit of the gods is within you, and that you have insight, intelligence, and outstanding wisdom. None of my people could read this writing and tell me its meaning. If you can do it, I will richly reward you with power and fortune."**

(Daniel shakes his head.) **Daniel replies, "I do not want your rewards. Nevertheless, I will translate God's words. God gave your father, King Nebuchadnezzar, power and splendor, yet Nebuchadnezzar became arrogant and hardened with pride.** (Daniel swaggers.) **Then God threw Nebuchadnezzar down from his throne** (Daniel throws himself down), **stripped him of his glory, and caused him for seven years to have mental illness. Finally, Nebuchadnezzar came to his senses and acknowledged the Most High God.** (Daniel stands up and points at Belshazzar.) **You, Belshazzar, his son, knew all these things, but you have not humbled yourself. Instead, you arrogantly set yourself up against the Lord of heaven.** (Daniel swaggers while pointing up.) **You committed sacrilege with the holy vessels of gold and silver from the temple in Jerusalem.** (Daniel points at the cups.) **You committed idolatry by praising non-existent gods. You did not honor the true God who** holds your life in his hand. Therefore, God himself wrote this inscription: (Daniel traces the words vertically with the yardstick) Numbered, numbered, weighed, divided. The meaning of 'numbered' (Daniel holds up the yardstick) is God has numbered the days of your reign and brought them to an end. The meaning of 'weighed' (Daniel balances the yardstick on the edge of his hand) is you have been weighed on God's scales, and you failed the test. The meaning of 'divided' (Daniel breaks the yardstick in half) is your kingdom is divided and given to your enemies."

(The lights are turned off, and the clowns exit.) True to his word, King Belshazzar, gave Daniel a reward. However, the king still failed to heed the warning of God's grim graffiti. That very night King Belshazzar was killed, and a foreign power conquered his kingdom.

From this story comes the expression "reading the handwriting on the wall." Let *us* do that more faithfully and successfully than did King Belshazzar.

Daring Daniel, the Lion Tamer

Theme: Faith, suffering, courage, salvation.

Cast: Narrator and three or more clowns.

Level: Children.

Props: Crown, scepter, white robe/wings, fur coat/carpet fragments/paper mane, signs ("ROAR" and "PURR"), magnifying glass, rope, banner ("PRAISE TO THE LIVING GOD").

The Performance

(The Narrator gathers the children in a group and begins.) **Who knows what a lion tamer is?** (The children answer.) **We have a story this morning about the greatest lion tamer ever. His name was Daniel. Daniel didn't work in a great circus and didn't use a whip and a chair, because his faith in God tamed the lions.**

To tell Daniel's story, each one of us has a part to play. (The Narrator recruits one child to play the part of the Angel. That child is given a white robe or paper wings to wear. Two or three children will be lions. They are given fur coats, plush carpet fragments, or paper "manes" to wear. The rest of the children form the lion's den by linking hands in a circle. The "lions" are inside the "den." The Narrator and the "Angel" stand outside the circle.)

Okay, lions, what do lions sound like? (Children roar.) **Good. When I hold up this sign** (the sign reads "ROAR"), **I want to hear the lions. Now we can begin our story.**

("King Darius" clown, wearing an exaggerated yellow paper crown, enters.) **Long ago a king named Darius lived in a country called Persia.** The country was too big for King Darius to rule directly, so he divided his country into 120 sections. (Darius slices the congregation into groups with his hand or fake scepter.) **Each section was ruled by a governor.** ("Governor" clowns and "Daniel" clown enter and stand in front of different groups.) **The 120 governors were led by three presidents.**

One of the three presidents chosen by King Darius was Daniel. (Darius puts his hand on Daniel.) **Daniel soon proved himself better than all the other presidents and governors. He had such great ability that the king thought about making him his supreme assistant to govern the whole country.** (Darius sweeps his arm across the whole sanctuary.)

That made some of the governors jealous of Daniel. (The governors gather together in a group, whispering to each other, and pointing to Daniel.) **They looked for some fault in the way he did business—but they found nothing they could criticize!** (The governors look at Daniel with a huge magnifying glass and scratch their heads.) **Daniel was faithful and honest, and he made no mistakes. They decided the only way to get rid of Daniel was through his religion—which they didn't like much anyway.**

(The governors go to Darius with a huge piece of paper and a giant pen.) **So the governors went to King Darius and said, "O great king, we think you should make a law honoring yourself. Make a law that for the next 30 days, people may pray only to you. A person praying to anyone or anything else shall be thrown to the lions.** (The governors point to the lions, and the Narrator holds up the sign "ROAR.") **We ask that you sign this law so that it cannot be changed."**

Well, the king was so flattered that he gladly signed the law. (Darius acts flattered and signs the paper.) **Oh, the king was going to regret that!**

When news of the law reached Daniel, he knew that such a law was wrong. It was a human law that broke God's law. Daniel decided to follow God's law no matter what the consequences were. (Daniel goes to a window or to the altar, kneels, and prays.) **He went home to his upstairs bedroom window that faced Jerusalem, his home city, and prayed as he usually did. He gave thanks to God, even though he knew that doing so might mean that he would be thrown to the lions.** (The Narrator holds up the sign).

The governors were waiting and watching. (The governors point at him.) **When they saw Daniel praying, they rushed to the king. They said to him, "Oh King, you signed an unchangeable law that for thirty days no one could pray except to you.** (They show him the paper.) **Anyone breaking this law must be thrown to the lions.** (The Narrator holds up the sign). **Daniel has broken the law, and now he must die."**

The king became very upset. He liked Daniel, and he was very sorry he had signed that stupid law. He spent all day trying to think of some way to save Daniel, but he could not. (Darius paces and scratches his head.) **In the evening he gave the order to arrest Daniel and take him to the lions' den.** (The Narrator holds up the sign).

The king said to him, "Daniel, may the god you worship save you now." Then they threw Daniel in with the lions. (The governors push Daniel into the circle formed by the children. The Narrator holds up the sign.) **They sealed the den with a huge stone so that no human could rescue Daniel.** (Governors close the circle of children, move off some distance, and turn their backs toward the children.)

But Daniel was safe in the lion's den. (The Narrator holds up sign.) **To protect Daniel, God sent an angel down into the den, and the angel tamed the lions.** (The Narrator guides the Angel into the circle between Daniel and the lion children. Daniel kneels. The Narrator whispers to the lions to lie down and pretend to sleep.) **The lions were now just big pussycats.** (The Narrator holds up a sign that reads "PURR.")

Meanwhile, back at the palace, the king didn't know that Daniel was safe. Thinking Daniel would probably be killed, the king was so sad that he went to bed without supper and didn't sleep all night. (Darius lies on floor, but tosses and turns.) **As soon as the sun rose the next morning, the king leaped out of bed, raced to the lion's den, and shouted, "O Daniel, was your god, whom you always worship, able to save you from the lions?"**

And Daniel answered, "O great king, my God sent an angel to protect me from the lions. I am without even a scratch. God rescued me because I am innocent of any wrongdoing against him or against you."

The king ordered his servants to remove the large stone and lift Daniel from the den. (Darius opens the circle of children, throws Daniel a rope, and pulls him out of the circle.) **The king was filled with joy to see Daniel unhurt.** (Darius and Daniel hug. The Narrator guides the Angel back out of the circle and whispers to the lions to get back up.)

Then the king ordered, "I command that those evil men who accused Daniel be thrown into the den of lions." (Darius points at the startled governor clowns. The Narrator holds up the "ROAR" sign.)

Well, the angel had left, and the hungry lions were no longer pussycats. The evil governors were thrown into the den, and before they even hit the floor the lions leaped upon them and ate them all up. (The governors throw themselves with mock horror unto the floor of the circle by the lions.)

Then the king sent to everyone in the country a message praising the one true God who had saved Daniel from the lions. (Darius unfurls a banner that says "PRAISE TO THE LIVING GOD.")

Naughty Nineveh and the Proud Pharisees

Theme: Repentance, Lent.

Cast: Narrator and three or more clowns.

Level: Adult.

Props: Chairs, robe, fake sword, cardboard "whale," signs ("REPENT," "RELIGIOUS LAW/NO HEART"), large burlap bag or paper sack, plate.

The Performance

(The "King" clown, wearing a brightly colored robe or coat, and a fake sword in his belt, sits on a chair. One or more clowns kneel before him. As the Narrator begins, the "Jonah" clown enters.)

You all remember the story of Jonah and the whale. God told Jonah to go preach to the city of Nineveh. (Jonah stops, cups his hand to his ear, points at the King, shakes his head, and walks another direction.) **But Jonah disobeyed. He boarded a boat headed in the opposite direction.** (Jonah stands on a chair.) **During a terrible storm, he was tossed into the sea and was swallowed by a whale.** (Jonah falls off chair. He lies in front of a large cardboard cutout of a whale. Alternately, two or three other clowns pick him up and carry him.) **Inside the whale's belly, Jonah had an attitude adjustment. He was sorry about trying to run from God** (Jonah prays), **and God gave Jonah another chance. God made the whale spit Jonah out on the beach, and Jonah headed for Nineveh.** (Jonah rolls out of the "whale," or the other clowns drop him on the floor.)

97

We all know the story about the whale, but the following story about what happened at Nineveh is less familiar. Nineveh was not a nice place for a Jewish boy like Jonah. Nineveh was the capitol city of Assyria, Israel's cruelest enemy. ("King" clown waves his sword and slaps the other clowns kneeling before him. They cower.) Nineveh was an evil and violent city. No wonder Jonah was afraid to go there. He thought that he would probably be killed, as other prophets had been. (Jonah walks to the other clowns.) But Jonah was not killed. Instead, an amazing change happened.

Jonah preached to the people that God was going to destroy the city in forty days. (Jonah shakes his finger at the others and holds up a large sign "RE-PENT!") Jonah's simple message was the single most successful evangelistic crusade in history. One hundred and twenty thousand people believed God, and they were very sorry for all the terrible things they had done. (Clowns beat their chests and pray.)

Even the king was sorry. The king stripped off his beautiful robe and gold. He put on sackcloth, a cheap, rough cloth that was a symbol of sorrow and repentance. (The King takes off his fancy coat and puts on a burlap or paper sack.). The king left the fancy throne that was a symbol of his power, and sat in a heap of ashes. (The king sits on the floor.) The king, accustomed to the finest feasts, declared a national fast, a time when no one would eat anything. (The King refuses a plate of food offered by another clown). The king, who had led his people in bloody conquests, now led his people in renouncing and rejecting their violent and evil ways. (The King throws down his sword and turns his back on it.)

Because the people of Nineveh had changed, God changed the city's fate. There was no longer any reason to destroy the city. God let them live. (Clowns look up with relief, hug each other, and celebrate.) Many, many years passed. (Clowns lie on the floor as if buried in a cemetery. "Pharisee" clowns enter and walk with their noses in the air.) During the time of Jesus, some of the religious leaders were called the Pharisees. The Pharisees *seemed* to be the opposite of the ancient, cruel people of Nineveh. The Pharisees were very religious. (A Pharisee clown holds up the sign, "RELIGIOUS LAW.") They observed religion down to the last letter of the law (A Pharisee clown counts the letters) and taught the laypeople to do the same. But what the Pharisees had in *form* they did not have in *essence*. (Pharisee clown turns his sign around. It has a drawing of a heart with a large slash through it.) They knew the *letter* of the law, but not the *spirit*. They were hypocrites. They acted out of pride, greed, and self-righteousness, rather than true love of God. They also were *not* sorry for the things they did wrong. (Pharisees shake their heads.)

Jesus said that on the great day of judgment, the people of Nineveh will rise up and condemn the Pharisees and the people like them. (Nineveh clowns stand up and point fingers at the Pharisee clowns. The Pharisee clowns shudder and cower in fear.) The people of Nineveh heard the preaching of Jonah and repented, but the Pharisees heard the preaching of Jesus—someone far greater than Jonah—and yet they did not repent. (All the clowns face away from the audience.)

The proud, hypocritical, self-righteous Pharisees did *not* repent. The barbaric, violent, evil people of

Nineveh *did* repent. Now—what about us? (Clowns all turn and mime "Who, me?")

Nineveh repented of its violence. Every day we hear news reports of some violent crime. (Two clowns pretend to beat another clown.) Every day people commit murders, robberies, assaults, and other violent acts. Do such people need to repent?

Many people would never rob or murder another person, yet they are abusive and damaging in more subtle ways. Many people gossip about others, argue with others, lack compassion toward others, and take advantage of others. (Clowns pantomime gossip, arguments, and indifference.) These are all forms of verbal and mental violence. Do such people need to repent?

Some people have no use for religion. They have many excuses for not becoming part of a church. (Clowns all leave for a moment.) Do such people need to repent?

Some people attend church every Wednesday and twice on Sunday. (Clowns all rush in and stand or sit around the pulpit.) Some are leaders of those churches. But none live up to what they teach or are taught. Do such people need to repent?

The answer to all these questions is: Yes! (Clowns hold up "REPENT" sign.) Like the people of Nineveh, some violence and lack of true faith exists in all of us. Like the Pharisees, some hypocrisy, greed, and pride exists in all of us. (Clowns point at themselves and nod in agreement.) Those who *feel* no need to repent, *need* to repent most of all.

GOSPELS

Follow That Star!

Theme: Christmas.

Cast: Narrator and two or more clowns.

Level: Children/adult.

Props: Book, binoculars or telescope, tinsel or foil, play money, riding horse or saw horse, potato chips and Coke can, crown, robe, juggling balls, doll, pouch, two bottles, many paper stars.

The Performance

("Wiseman" clown, reading a book as he walks, enters as the Narrator begins.) **Long, long ago, in a country far, far to the east, lived some very smart people called "wisemen" or "magi." They were wealthy men educated in philosophy, religion, science, and astronomy.**

One night they noticed a very bright star in the sky. ("Star" clown enters, dancing, and shaking arms that have tinsel on them. The Wiseman clown looks at him with binoculars or a small telescope.) **They watched it every night. The star got brighter and moved in relation to the other stars.** (Star clown dances faster and moves around.) **The wisemen decided the star must be a sign from God. God was telling them that a great king was born!**

They wanted to go worship the new king! They bought camels and supplies to last the long trip. (Wiseman pulls out play money. He brings out the rocking horse or saw horse. He puts a backpack or sack over his shoulder and gets on the horse). **They climbed on their camels and off they went on their great journey!**

They traveled during the cool evenings and nights, always following the star. (Star gestures "come on" as he walks around in front of the other clown on the rocking horse.) **In the mornings they ate and drank.** (Star hides. Wiseman gets off horse and takes out Coke and potato chips from a sack.) **During the hot afternoons they slept in the shade of their camels.** (Wiseman curls up on the ground nearby.) **Every day the camels seemed to smell worse.** (Wiseman holds his nose.) **Sometimes in the evenings, the camels did not feel like traveling. The wisemen had to push, plead, and pull the camels.** (Wiseman pushes the horse, pulls, and gets on his knees.) **Finally, they would be on their way again.** (Wiseman gets back on the horse.)

After many months of difficult traveling they came to Jerusalem, the capital city of Judea. They asked to speak with King Herod. (Star puts on a crown and assumes the character of Herod.) **He would surely know where the new king of the Jews was born.**

But Herod was surprised and did not know. (Star/Herod acts surprised and momentarily turns his back on the wiseman.) **Herod asked his own priests and teachers. They told him the Christ was to be born in Bethlehem.** (Star/Herod turns around.)

Herod told them they would find the child in Bethlehem—only six miles away. (Wiseman smiles and claps his hands.) **The wisemen were very happy because they had almost reached their goal.**

King Herod asked them to return with news of

the new king. He said that he also wanted to worship the Christ. But Herod lied. (Star/Herod frowns and hides.) He wanted to kill the new king, not worship him.

The wisemen hopped on their camels and off they went. (Wiseman gets on horse and spurs him on, but then realizes he's going the wrong direction and turns the camel around.) Where was the star? To the right? To the left? (From his hiding place, Star sticks out an arm, then a leg, then his whole self.) There it was! They followed the star the few remaining miles to Bethlehem. When they reached Bethlehem, the star was directly over a motel's barn. Could a great king be in a barn full of animals?

Leaping from their camels, the wisemen ran inside, finding Mary and the child, Jesus. (Star clown throws on a robe on top of his head to become Mary and picks up a doll.) When the wisemen saw the little Jesus, they knew he was the great king. (Wiseman gets on his knees and frantically looks through his bag for the gifts.) They worshiped Jesus, and gave him gold . . . (Wiseman can't find the gold.) GOLD! . . . (Wiseman triumphantly holds up pouch, and gives it to Star/Mary. Then he gives her two bottles.) frankincense, an expensive air freshener, and myrrh, a sweet smelling perfume.

After worshiping the new king, the wisemen happily left to return home. (Wiseman goes back and lies beside his camel.) That night God warned the wisemen in a dream not to go back to Herod, but to return directly home. (Star whispers in Wiseman's ear. Wiseman hops back on horse.) As they traveled home, the Wisemen thought back on their long journey of sand, cold, heat, and uncertainty. Had the trip been worth it? (Wiseman nods.) **Oh yes, to see the king was worth it all.**

(The clowns distribute paper stars.) **To help you remember the wisemen's journey following the star and their joy upon finding the new king, we have a star for each one of you.**

The Eternal Eternally-New Good News

Theme: Creativity, tradition, New Year's.

Cast: Narrator and two or more clowns.

Level: Adult.

Props: Signs ("OLD"/"TRADITION," "NEW"/"CRE-ATIVITY," two each of "GOSPEL" and "1990's"), tape, sponge or brush, bottle or jug.

The Performance

(The Narrator begins.) **Jesus was once asked why the Pharisees and John's disciples practiced certain religious customs, but Jesus and his disciples did not. In his answer, Jesus described how the eternally-new good news that he brought into the world could not be contained in the old, tradition-bound religion of the day.**

(Two clowns with signs around their necks enter. One sign says "Old," the other clown's sign says "New.") **Jesus used the example of placing a patch of new cloth on an old pair of pants.** ("New" clown places a large piece of tape on the posterior of the "Old" clown. Old clown turns around so that everyone can see the tape patch on his pants, and pretends to wash himself with a sponge or scrub brush.) **In the age before permanent press fabrics, a new piece of cloth shrank a lot when it was washed. When an old pants with a new patch was washed, the new cloth shrank, tearing the old cloth even more.** (New clown secretly but

---

*Supporting scripture: Mark 2:18-22, Luke 5:33-39.

loudly rips a piece of cloth or paper. Old clown drops the sponge, grabs his patch and looks embarrassed.)

Jesus also used the example of new wine and wineskins. In the days before glass and plastic bottles, skins of sheep or goats were sewn together to contain liquid. Freshly made wine was poured into a fresh, new skin. (A third clown or the Narrator pretends to pour from a large bottle or jug labeled "New Wine" into New clown's mouth.) **The new wine was still fermenting and producing gas, but the new wineskin was still flexible and elastic enough to stretch under the pressure of the fermentation.** (New clown stretches, pretends to "swell," makes smooth circles with his arms, smiles, and freezes in position.)

An old wineskin, on the other hand, was only good for storing water or aged wine because the wineskin had lost its original flexibility and elasticity. (Old clown looks offended by the insult and motions for the Narrator or third clown to pour some "New Wine" into him. Reluctantly, the Narrator or clown does.) **If new wine were poured into an old wineskin, the fermenting wine would put pressure on the brittle old wineskin, causing the wineskin to burst!** (Old clown, keeping his arms straight down at his sides, begins to shake and jerk. He stretches a little, but then "bursts" and falls on the ground.)

So it is with the eternal, eternally-new good news of Jesus Christ. The gospel is eternal because God is eternal. But it is also always new to meet the needs of people in every age. (While Narrator reads this section, the clowns turn over the labels around their necks. New clown's label now is "Creativity," and Old clown's label is now "Tradition." Both clowns pick up and hold in

one hand individual signs that both read "GOSPEL."
Both clowns smile. Then, in their remaining hands, both
pick up signs that say "1990's" or the current year.
With a sign in each hand, Creative clown begins dancing
energetically, looking happy and alive. However, with a
sign in each hand, Tradition clown frowns and makes
slow, jerky movements in an awkward dance.) **The
ever-creative, eternally-new gospel of Jesus burst the
old forms and traditions of his day. And so it is in
every age. The eternal gospel must take on new forms
and structures to meet the needs of every generation.
God's good news is eternal, but people's structures
and forms grow old and must change in order to
hold the new wine of the gospel. Nevertheless, just as
Jesus did not throw out all his Old Testament roots,
churches today need both tradition and creativity.**
(The two clowns now join hands and dance together.
Creative clown dances more calmly than before; Tradition clown, more smoothly.) **Churches need tradition
to provide a sense of history, belonging, and continu-
ity. Tradition provides bearings for the future in an
unbalanced, ever-accelerating world. But churches
need creativity to keep tradition from becoming a god
in themselves, to communicate the gospel in meaning-
ful ways in a changing society, and to give us new
energy and life.** (Clowns dance out.)

Pennies for Heaven

Theme: Stewardship, sacrifice.

Cast: Narrator and two clowns.

Level: Children/adult.

Props: Twinkie, Monopoly money, sign ("CATHE-DRAL"), small bag, offering plate, table, horn, feather duster, chair, pennies.

The Performance

(On one side of the room hangs a sign "CATHE-DRAL." Nearby is an offering plate on a small table. About five feet from the table is a chair. The "rich" clown enters and the Narrator begins.) **There once was a rich man who had everything he wanted. He had all the finest clothes** (clown puts on a stupid hat and shows off his clothes), **and the finest house** (clown raises his arms to make an imaginary square), **and the finest food** (clown takes a bite out of a Twinkie).

One day the rich man decided to go to the cathe-dral, a very large church, to give his gift to God. (Clown pulls out Monopoly money.) **He would give some hundred dollar bills and even a thousand dollar bill—that would really shock people! Then everyone would know what a good person he was.** (Clown looks very pleased with himself and straightens his tie.)

He put his offering money in a little bag (clown does so), **but, of course, he left plenty behind so that he could keep his wonderful life just as it was.** (Clown stuffs the rest of the money back in his pocket).

*Supporting scripture: Luke 21:1-4.

(Clown walks over to the "CATHEDRAL" sign, points at it, and looks around.) **When he got to the cathedral, he looked around to see if people were watching him.** (Clown blows his horn, bows to the people, and elaborately places the money in the offering plate. Then he looks up at the ceiling with his hands together in a prayer position.) **Happy with himself and his great generosity, the rich man sat down.** (Clown dusts the chair off with his feather duster or hat, and sits down.) **He wanted to watch what others were putting into the plate.**

("Widow" clown enters.) **As he was sitting there, a widow lady came in. She was very poor.** (Widow clown pulls out her pockets to show that they are empty.) **Her husband had died, and she had a hard time finding work.**

The rich man asked himself, what was she (Rich clown points at her) **doing here? She had no money. She must be planning to steal from the offering plate, he thought.** (Rich clown leans forward, suspiciously.) **The rich man watched carefully. She was getting closer and closer to the money—his money—in the offering plate.** (Widow clown comes closer, stretching out her hand. Rich clown is nearly falling off the edge of his chair.) **She reached out her hand and . . .** (Widow clown drops two pennies into offering plate.) **Hey! Instead of taking money, she dropped two pennies into the offering plate.**

The rich man began to laugh. (Rich clown laughs and falls off his chair.) **Why that was only two cents worth! Almost nothing at all! God would certainly be more pleased with his gift than with hers.** (Rich clown stands up and strikes a pompous pose. Widow

clown bows her head. Both freeze in position.)
Now I have a question for all of you. Which one did Jesus say gave the most? (The Narrator points to Rich clown, then to Widow clown.)
What about the rich man? He gave more than a thousand dollars, but he had much more left over. (Rich clown shows money in his pockets.) **He gave only a fraction of his wealth.**

What about the poor widow? She gave only two cents, but she had nothing left over. (Widow clown shows her empty pockets.) **She gave everything she had.**

Jesus said the poor widow gave the most. (Rich clown looks horrified and then, humiliated, shuffles out. Widow clown looks surprised, then smiles. The Narrator pats her shoulder.) **Even though she had very little, she gave all that she owned. The rich man gave his bills for his own glory. The widow gave her pennies for heaven.**

In God's eyes, giving is measured not by the amount given, but by the amount kept back; not by the exact count, but by one's attitude; not by the glory, but by the sacrifice.

Today, we have a penny for each one of you to help you remember the poor widow giving everything to God. (The Narrator and Widow clown distribute pennies.)

Shepherd Saves Silly Sheep

Luke 15:1-7

Theme: Sin, salvation.

Cast: Narrator and two 2 clowns.

Level: Children/adult.

Props: Two signs ("99 SHEEP," and "Save Our Sheep" the first letters of the second sign are much larger than the rest of the words so that SOS is clearly noticable), umbrella (with curved handle), bell, 7-Up cans, fake binoculars, huge sunglasses, flashlight, party poppers, horn or noisemaker, cotton balls.

The Performance

(The Narrator talks to the children gathered at the front.) **You have a special part in today's story. You get to pretend to be sheep. We are going to pretend here in this group that we have 99 sheep. What would 99 sheep sound like? Let's hear the 99 sheep "baa" now.** (Children baa.) **That's good. Every time I hold up this sign** (holds up the sign that reads "99 SHEEP") **you all talk like sheep. Remember, only when I hold up the sign. Let's start our story.**

Once a shepherd owned 100 sheep. (The "Shepherd" clown, carrying a folded umbrella upside-down as if it were a shepherd's crook, enters. The "Sheep" clown crawls in on all fours.) **The good shepherd owned 99** (the Narrator holds up the sign and children baa) **well-behaved sheep that did everything the shepherd wanted them to do, and he owned one naughty sheep that often got into trouble.** (Sheep clown butts the Narrator.)

112

On hot days (Shepherd dons a pair of huge sun-glasses and fans himself with his hat) **the shepherd would take his 99 sheep** (the Narrator holds up the sign) **and the one silly sheep to get a cool drink from the stream.** (Shepherd puts a six-pack of empty 7-UP cans near the children.) **The naughty sheep would butt her way to the front of the line and not let any other sheep get a drink.** (Sheep crouches possessively over all of the cans. Shepherd pulls the Sheep away from the cans with his umbrella's crook, and shakes his finger at her.) **The shepherd would have to stop the naughty sheep, so that the 99 sheep** (the Narrator holds up the the sign) **could get a drink from the stream.**

When the shepherd would take his sheep to a field filled with luscious green grass to eat, the 99 sheep (the Narrator holds up the sign) **followed him, but the naughty sheep often went the other way.** (The Shepherd points and walks in one direction. Sheep crawls rapidly in the opposite direction. The Shepherd looks back over his shoulder, runs back to the Sheep, grabs her with the crook of his umbrella, and points the Sheep in the proper direction.) **When the shepherd made her go in the right direction with the 99 sheep** (the Narrator holds up the sign), **the silly sheep would pout and whine all day.** (Sheep pouts.)

Even though the silly sheep did many bad things, the shepherd still loved her just like he loved all his sheep. (The Shepherd pats or hugs Sheep.)

One evening, the shepherd rang his bell (Shepherd rings a bell) **to call all the sheep** (the Narrator holds up the sign) **into their pens, where they would be safe from wolves, bears, lions, and other dangers.** (Sheep slips away and crawls up on a pew or platform where she can be easily seen.) **The shepherd began counting**

his sheep. One, two, three, (Shepherd mimes counting the children) **four, five . . . until he got up to 99.** (The Narrator holds up the sign.) **Oh, no! The shepherd owned 100 sheep, not just 99.** (The Narrator holds up the sign.) **One sheep was missing! Which one was it?** (Sheep waves.) **The naughty sheep, of course.**

The good shepherd began to worry. He knew all the harmful things that might hurt the missing sheep. What would he do? The shepherd would go and find her, because each and every one of his sheep was special to him. (Shepherd begins walking around, pretending to be searching. He uses fake binoculars with huge eyeballs painted on the ends.)

Soon the sun went down, and everything got very dark. (Shepherd pulls a flashlight from his pocket.) **Then rain began to fall** (Shepherd feels imaginary rain drops, and transforms his staff into an umbrella), **the lightning flashed, and the thunder cracked** (Sheep explodes a party popper)!

Meanwhile, the naughty sheep was lost, wet, cold, and scared! (Sheep shivers.) **Why did she wander off? She wanted to see what was over the hill, but she found only rocks and thorns.** (Sheep pretends to prick her hoof on a thorn.) **No good green grass at all. Now she was lost and cold and caught in some thorns. She might never find home again. A wolf or bear might eat her. Things were looking very . . .** (Sheep finishes the Narrator's sentence by bleating, "BAAAAAD").

Now she was sorry. She was sorry for running away. She was sorry for all the bad things she had ever done. If only some help would come. (Sheep holds up the "S.O.S.")

After many hours of searching, the good shepherd was tired and numb from the cold. (Shepherd staggers, leans on the folded umbrella, and shivers.) **But look!** (Shepherd leaps up excitedly, and Sheep starts waving at him.) **There was the little lost sheep! The shepherd joyfully ran over and reached out with his shepherd's staff to save the sheep.** (Shepherd reaches out the umbrella. Sheep grabs the umbrella, then leaps into the Shepherd's arms. The Shepherd honks a horn, and they dance back to the children.)

The sheep was so happy to be back that she never again ran away from the shepherd. She also became better friends with the 99 sheep. (The Narrator holds up the sign, children baa, Sheep hugs various children.) **And that also made the good shepherd happy.** (Shepherd nods head.)

Does this story of the silly sheep remind you of anybody? People are like that lost sheep, and God is like that good shepherd. We often don't do what God wants for us. We often choose things that will later hurt us. Yet, God, our good shepherd, still loves us so much that he wants to save us from the trouble we get in.

To help you remember the story, we are giving each one of you a white ball of cotton that looks just like the white wool of a little lost sheep. (Shepherd and Sheep begin handing out cotton balls to the children.)

The Tale of Ten Troubled People

Theme: Thanksgiving.

Cast: Narrator and three or more clowns.

Level: Children/adult.

Props: Wilted flower, "D" on a paper, horns, noisemakers.

The Performance

We've all had various problems in our lives A problem may seem very bad at the time, yet if someone helps us solve that problem, are we thankful? Jesus once helped out some people who were not very thankful. That story goes something like this.

Ten (or however many clowns are available enter) troubled people heard that Jesus was coming to their town. Among the ten were a farmer whose crops had failed (one clown holds up a wilted flower), a student who got nothing but D's (another clown holds up a sheet of paper with a big red "D" drawn on the top), and a kid whose mom was always getting mad at him for getting his clothes so dirty (another clown brushes off his clothes and cringes).

These troubled people parked their cars and bicycles on the highway leading into town and waited for Jesus. (All of the clowns form a line across the front.)

When they saw him they honked their horns (clowns use horns and noisemakers to make a racket), and they yelled, "Jesus, sir, help us, for we have many problems!" (The Narrator walks toward them.)

Jesus said simply, "Go talk to a pastor." (The Narrator points down an aisle or out a door. The clowns look at each other, then start walking in the indicated direction.)

As they drove to a church, they were all struck with good ideas about how to solve their primary problems (each clown raises an index finger and mimes discovery as they walk away): how to plant better crops, how to study better, how to keep out of the dirt.

One person turned his car around. (One clown returns, pretending to drive around looking for the Narrator.) He found Jesus eating lunch in McDonald's. In front of the cooks and customers the person shouted, "Praise God! Praise the Lord! Thank you, Jesus! Thank you!" (Clown kneels before Narrator and shakes his hand vigorously.) This person was a _____ (fill in the blank with a person of bad reputation in your own situation, such as Nazi, Communist, Ku Klux Klan member, gang member, cult member.)

Jesus asked, "Didn't I help ten (or whatever number) people? Where are the nine _____ (fill in with the name of your own denomination or congregation)? Why did none return to thank me except this _____?" (Clown shrugs.)

And Jesus said to the man, "Go on your way—your faith has helped you with your trouble."

A Morning Like This?

Theme:. Friendship, suffering, resurrection, Easter.

Cast: Narrator and two or more clowns.

Level: Children/adult.

Props: Large silk rose, Band-Aid, Wonder Bread, Bible, red magic marker, "tomb" made from a table and white sheets, perfume, large handkerchief, tape of "Was It A Morning Like This?" by Croegaert and Patti, helium balloons, sign ("JESUS IS RISEN").

The Performance

(The Narrator calls the children to the front for a children's story. After the children gather, the clown "Mary" enters and wanders along the edge of the congregation.) **To celebrate Easter we have a very special story for you this morning, but I need some help in telling it.**

(The Narrator looks around, notices the clown, and calls to her.) **Hey, Clown, would you help me tell a story?** (Mary points to herself.) **Yes. It's a story about a morning like this many years ago** (Mary shyly shakes her head.) **But we need you. You would be Mary Magdalene in one of the greatest stories ever told. Will you help?** (Mary considers the proposition longer this time, but again shyly shakes her head. Carrying a large silk rose, the "Jesus" clown enters from behind the Narrator. Mary notices that, like her, Jesus has the marks of a clown on his face. Jesus tips his hat

*Supporting scripture: John 19:25-42, 20:1-18.

118

to her and offers her the rose. She accepts it and follows him to the front.)

Good, let's begin our story. Mary Magdalene (the Narrator points to Mary) **was a good friend of Jesus** (the Narrator points to Jesus, who puts his arm around Mary's shoulders). **Jesus was Mary's Hero. Jesus healed the sick.** (Frowning, Mary holds her limp wrist as if it hurt. Jesus puts a large Band-Aid on it, and Mary smiles.) **He taught people about God.** (Jesus points to the ceiling and to a Bible, and then stretches his hands to the congregation.) **He fed the hungry people who came to listen to him.** (Jesus hands out slices of Wonder Bread to the children.) **He wanted to show God's love to everyone.** (Jesus points to the ceiling, then to his heart, and then to the congregation.)

But some people did not like what Jesus was doing. (Jesus sadly shakes his head.) **They hated him. One Friday, these people grabbed him and nailed him to a cross.** (Jesus mimes being nailed to a cross. The congregation now sees on Jesus' outstretched palms red spots previously applied with a marker. Mary is stunned. Jesus sadly gazes at Mary and the entire congregation.) **As Jesus hung on the cross, Mary stood nearby.** (Mary sobs into a huge handkerchief.) **Mary watched as, after many painful hours, Jesus finally died.** (Jesus looks upward for a moment and then drops his head so that his hat falls off. Mary drops to her knees, weeping. Mary picks up the hat and begins to walk away.)

Wait, Clown! That's not the end of the story We still need you. (Mary returns, but continues to cry.) **One of Jesus' followers took the body, and laid it in a tomb.** (Someone from the congregation or another clown drags Jesus to the tomb made of a table and white

119

sheets. Mary follows. She places Jesus' hat over his face and the rose on his chest. A sheet is pulled down over the table, hiding Jesus from view. Jesus sneaks out the back of the table, leaving the rose in the tomb. Mary sits forlornly.) **Because Jesus was dead and buried, his followers were terribly sad. On the following Sunday morning, Mary Magdalene** (Mary does not hear at first) . . . **Mary Magdalene, following the customs of her day, went to put perfume on the dead body of Jesus.** (The Narrator gives Mary the bottle of perfume. She sprays some in the air and sniffs it.) **This would be her final act of love for Jesus.**

(Mary goes to the tomb, lifts up the front sheet, and discovers the tomb is empty except for the rose.) **Look, the body of Jesus is no longer there!** (Mary takes the rose. Puzzled, she looks at the Narrator and motions "Where is he?" Confused, angry, and grief-stricken, Mary again begins to leave.) **Please don't go. There's still more. Jesus is alive! Jesus is risen from the dead!**

(Mary does not believe the Narrator, and wants out of the story. She shakes her head, angrily throws the rose down, begins crying again, and slowly continues walking. A tape of "Was It A Morning Like This?", written and composed by Jim Croegaert and sung by Sandi Patti, is played at this point. Jesus re-enters, picks up the rose, walks up behind Mary, and offers her the rose again. Mary looks up in amazement, then joyously rushes into his arms. Several helium balloons, tied to a sign "JESUS IS RISEN," are stored behind the tomb. Jesus and Mary release the balloons, which carry the sign up to the ceiling. Jesus and Mary joyfully dance out of the sanctuary in time with the music.)

Were You There?

Theme: Easter.

Cast: Narrator and two or more clowns.

Level: Adult.

Props: None needed, but a large wooden cross might be helpful.

The Performance

(A choir sings the hymn "Were You There" while the clowns act out the drama. All actions are done in slow motion.)

Were you there when they crucified my Lord? Were you there when they crucified my Lord? Oh! Sometimes it causes me to tremble, tremble, tremble. Were you there when they crucified my Lord? (First clown walks in, stands in front of the congregation, and gestures, "Who? Me?" Clown playing Jesus enters and stands five to ten feet behind first clown. First clown turns around and expresses surprise.)

Were you there when they nailed him to the tree? Were you there when they nailed him to the tree? Oh! Sometimes it causes me to tremble, tremble, tremble. Were you there when they nailed him to the tree? (Jesus clown is dragged to the cross by unseen hands, or by other clowns who enter and then leave. Jesus stretches out his arms. The congregation sees red spots previously drawn on his palms with a red marker. First clown approaches, kneels, and cries.)

*Supporting scripture: Mark 15-16, Luke 15-16, John 19-20.

121

Were you there when they laid him in the grave?
Were you there when they laid him in the grave? Oh!
Sometimes it causes me to tremble, tremble, tremble.
Were you there when they laid him in the grave?
(First clown takes down the body of Jesus and lays him
on the floor. He goes to one side, kneels, and sobs with
his face in his hands.)

Were you there when he rose up from the dead?
Were you there when he rose up from the dead? Oh!
Sometimes it causes me to tremble, tremble, tremble.
Were you there when he rose up from the dead?
(Jesus gets up, smiling. He goes over to the first clown
who is still kneeling, and touches him. The first clown
is stunned. Jesus helps him to his feet, and they embrace joyfully. At the end, the clowns turn to the congregation and gesture for them to rise. The choir direc-
tor tells the congregation to join with the choir as they
sing the last verse of "Were You There" one more time.
The clowns inconspicuously slip out as the congregation
sings.)

Making Disciples

Matthew 28:19*

Theme: Evangelism, discipleship.

Cast: Narrator and two clowns.

Level: Adult.

Props: Sign ("DISCIPLE"), Bible.

The Performance

(The Narrator begins as the clowns enter.) **This is the story of two people who loved God and wanted everyone to know the good news of the gospel.** (Clowns stand, facing the congregation, on opposite sides of the front.)

Ernie ("Ernie" clown waves) **was an effective evangelist. Through his words and his deeds, people heard and saw the good news of Jesus Christ. Five people a year became believers.** (Ernie gets the first five people in the front row on his side to stand up. If these five people had been previously informed about what to expect, they will stand up more readily and serve as effective role models for those who will follow. You may adjust this number to fit the size of the audience.) **Ernie the evangelist was thrilled for these five people** (clown shakes their hands and hugs them), **but after their conversions he did not spend much time with them.** (Ernie moves off to new people.) **The five people started going to church on their own—well, some of them did.**

---

*Supporting scripture: 2 Timothy 2:2.

123

Doug ("Doug" clown waves) also wanted to help people to know God, but he had a slightly different method. He resolved to follow the command of Jesus, in Matthew 28:19, to "Go and make disciples of all nations." (Doug holds up a sign that says, "DIS-CIPLE.") Doug the discipler spent all his efforts on only one person. (Doug gets the first person on his side to stand up.) After that first person became a believer, Doug still spent a lot of time with him, taking him to church (Doug takes person by the arm and sweeps his hand around the church to "show" him around), studying the Bible together (Doug opens a Bible and shows the person a verse), praying with him (Doug mimes a prayer with head bowed and hands folded), and just being a good friend to him (Doug puts his arm around him).

After one year, Ernie the evangelist could count five converts, but Doug the discipler, only one (clowns count). Although one was still a very good number, Ernie with his five couldn't help but feel just a little bit smug. (Ernie points at Doug and then his converts. Polishing his fingernails on his coat, he smiles.)

At the end of the second year, Ernie had five more converts (Ernie gets five more people to stand up), and Doug had one more (Doug gets one more person to stand). But wait a minute! Doug's first disciple also brought one friend to know God. (Doug gets one person to stand beside the first person.) Doug's first disciple also brought his friend to church, studied the Bible with him, prayed with him, and was a good friend to him. Thus, on Doug's side four people knew the Lord. That was good, but not as impressive as the eleven people on Ernie's side.

These efforts went on year after year. Ernie won five new converts a year, while Doug and his disciples each made one new convert a year. (Clowns get the appropriate number of people to stand.) At the end of the third year, sixteen people were on Ernie's side and eight on Doug's side. At the end of the fourth year, twenty-one people were on Ernie's side and sixteen on Doug's side.

But at the end of the fifth year, twenty-six people were on Ernie's side, and thirty-two people on Doug's side. Doug's method had passed Ernie's method in number. Each year Ernie added five converts to his number, but the number of Doug's disciples doubled!

Then one day both Ernie and Doug died. (Clowns leave.) Ernie's efforts on earth stopped. However, Dough's disciples kept on growing long after his death.

Although evangelism is important, discipleship is also needed. A conversion experience is good; but it is only a beginning, not an end in itself. Jesus did more than evangelize during his ministry on earth. He made disciples. His disciples grew into the Church. If Jesus had not made disciples, there would be no church today. We must all become faithful disciples of Jesus Christ. We should also become disciplers of others, so that they may also know the good news.

ACTS

Acts 3:1-4:22 The Leaping Cripple

Theme: Healing, salvation, evangelism.

Cast: Narrator and three or more clowns.

Level: Adult.

Props: Big clock, tin cup, coins, pulpit or chair, paper heart, paper dove.

The Performance

(The Narrator begins as the "Cripple" clown crawls up the aisle, or is carried in by two other clowns. If carried in, the cripple is deposited at the front, and the other two clowns go behind the altar and pretend to pray.) **This is the story of a man long ago who was born physically disabled. He was never able to walk. For more than forty years he could do little real work. He lived on handouts and charity.**

Every day at three in the afternoon (Cripple clown points to large clock set at 3:00), **the traditional time for prayer, some men would carry him to a temple gate.** (Cripple stretches out his cup. Extra clowns walk by and toss coins into the cup.) **He begged for money there because people going into the temple to pray to God were more generous than at other times and places.**

One day, not long after Jesus had risen from the grave and had ascended into heaven, the apostles Peter and John went to the temple to pray. (Two clowns enter and stand beside Cripple clown, who holds out his tin cup toward them.) **They saw the man**

begging for money, but Peter and John had no money. (They turn out their empty pockets.)

Then Peter took the disabled man's hand and said, "I have no money, but what I have I give you. In the name of Jesus Christ of Nazareth, walk!" ("Peter" clown pulls the Cripple clown to his feet. Astonished, Cripple clown drops his tin cup, feels his legs with his hands, takes one cautious step, then another.) The cripple's legs, ankles, and feet had become as whole and strong as they were always meant to be. (Cripple clown begins to dance, jump, turn cartwheels, and lift hands toward the ceiling. He shakes hands with Peter and John, then hugs them. He runs up and down the aisles showing the congregation his healed legs.)

The former disabled person, walking, leaping, and praising God, went with Peter and John into the temple courts. (Other clowns gather around, or else the three clowns move into the congregation.) A crowd gathered around them. When all the people saw the man walking, leaping, and praising God, they were astonished at the miracle of healing.

Peter began to preach to the crowd. (Peter stands on a chair, or by a pulpit, and pretends to preach.) Peter gave credit to God for the miracle (Peter points up). Peter told the people the good news of Jesus Christ, who had been killed on a cross (Peter crosses his arms), but who had risen from the grave (Peter moves his arms from horizontal to vertical), and had ascended into heaven (Peter points up). The people believed in Jesus because of Peter's preaching, and because of the miraculous healing. The people were sorry for their past sins, and praised God for his

power and love. (All clowns raise their hands and look toward the ceiling.)

We can be very glad for the cripple who leaps. (Cripple leaps.) **After all, who of us is not crippled in some way?** (All clowns sweep their arms around the audience.) **We might not be crippled physically, with illness or disability.** (A clown holds his stomach and limps.) **But some of us may be crippled emotionally, with anger, fear, or despair.** (Another clown tears a paper heart in half and holds it to his chest.) **Some of us may be crippled spiritually with doubt, unrepentance, or apathy.** (Another clown tears the wing from a paper dove and holds the pieces to his chest.)

But Jesus loves cripples. Jesus offers us emotional and spiritual healing. Jesus offers us the chance for our crippled emotions and spirits to walk, leap, and praise God. (Clowns leave jumping and dancing.)

Miraculous Magical Acts

Acts 19:8-20

Theme: Healing, salvation, false religion.

Cast: Narrator and three or more clowns.

Level: Adult.

Props: Pulpit, crumpled paper, sheet, large handkerchief, crucifix, old books, trash can.

The Performance

(The Narrator begins as "Paul" clown enters and pretends to preach from behind a pulpit.) **In the very early history of the Church, we read about many miraculous magical acts. In the book of Acts, Paul preached and taught in the city of Ephesus for more than two years.** (Other clowns enter, and begin to jeer at Paul, and toss crumpled paper at him.) **For three months he preached in the Jewish synagogue, but the people in that synagogue were stubborn. They refused to believe, and they said nasty things about the Christians.** (Other clowns leave, gesturing and scowling.)

After much abuse, Paul left the synagogue (Paul moves his pulpit to the other side), **and rented a lecture hall from a philosophy teacher.** (Paul picks up a bed sheet and pretends to sew.) **To pay his expenses, Paul made tents. He worked each morning until the sun was hot, and most people took a nap.** (Paul wipes his forehead with a large handkerchief, folds up the sheet, and walks behind the pulpit.) **Then Paul went to the lecture hall to hold church meetings and classes.**

131

For two years the church grew, until everyone had heard of it. During this time God did extraordinary miracles through Paul. (Two clowns enter. One pretends to be sick. The other helps him stagger in. The sick clown lies on the floor while the other goes up to Paul and begs. Paul gives him his handkerchief, which is placed on the sick clown. The sick clown gets up and dances.) People even placed Paul's handkerchiefs on those who were sick or were possessed by demons, and they were cured. (All clowns leave.) The people in Ephesus were very superstitious. Everyone consulted astrologers and practiced magic. Everyone was afraid of things that go bump in the night. (One clown enters, hides his face, and hunches over. A couple of other clowns enter and stand near him. They hold up a crucifix and gesture as if commanding the clown.) A group of Jews tried to drive out evil spirits by using the name of Jesus—just as they had seen Paul do. The exorcists said, "In the name of Jesus, whom Paul preaches, I command you to come out." (The "possessed" clown stands up and points a finger back at the "exorcist" clowns.) But when they tried this, the evil spirit answered, "Jesus I know and Paul I know, but who are you?" (The possessed clown jumps at the others, pulling off their hats and jackets, and chases them out.) Then the possessed man jumped on them and beat them up. They ran out of the house naked and badly injured.

(Some clowns come back in carrying old books and cupping a hand behind an ear.) When the story of what happened spread, many people feared the Lord. (Clowns shake and bow toward a cross on the wall, or other representation of Jesus.) Many now believed, and confessed all the things they had done wrong. (Clowns look sad.) **Some who had practiced magic and sorcery burned all their books of magic.** (Some clowns throw old books in a trash can.) **And the word of the Lord spread widely around the land.** (The clowns all leave in different directions.)

This story may not seem to have much to do with modern life. We don't try to make Jesus a magic formula—or do we? When we have problems do we pray, "Oh God, come and fix this?" Is Jesus our Lord and Savior, or a magical band-aid? Do we think the act of going to church on Sunday will save us, even though we don't think about God during the rest of the week? Do we ever use the phrase "The Bible says . . ." as a weapon to win an argument? Do we ever use religion to get what we want?

Let us renounce false piety. Let us not use Jesus as a magic wand. Let us practice repentance, humility, and sincerity. Let us spread the mighty word of the Lord.

LETTERS

Don't Repay Dirt

Theme: Peace, revenge, reconciliation.

Cast: Narrator and two clowns.

Level: Children/adult.

Props: Clear glass pitcher of water, four clear drinking glasses, bag of dirt, bucket, table, posters with texts of Romans 12:17 and 12:21, sign ("I'M SORRY").

The Performance

(A clear glass pitcher full of water, four empty clear drinking glasses, and a bag of dirt are set on top of a table. The empty bucket is placed under or beside the table. Two clowns jog in from different directions, and the Narrator begins.) **A man went jogging under the hot summer sun.** (Clown 1 jogs in exaggerated motions, but moves slowly.) **Of course, all this activity made him very thirsty. He wished for a tall, cool glass of water.** (The Narrator takes the pitcher and fills two glasses two-thirds full of water. Clown 1 acts hot and tired. He stops jogging and watches closely as the Narrator fills the glasses. The Narrator indicates that one of the glasses is for Clown 1. Clown 1 claps his hands as he walks slowly toward the glass.)

But there was another man who was always playing mean tricks on others. (Clown 2 jogs by, quickly takes a handful of dirt from the bag, drops the dirt in one glass of water, and takes the other. Laughing, he sneaks a few feet away.) **He threw dirt in the thirsty man's water.** (Clown 1 reaches the table and

136

sadly examines the glass of dirty water.) **Oh, the poor thirsty man! What can he do now?**

(Clown 1 gets angry and throws another handful of dirt into the glass.) **He could get angry and throw more dirt into his water. Maybe that would help release some of his anger, but that does not help solve the problem.** (Clown 1's anger disappears, and he shakes his head.)

He could get angry and throw dirt into the other jogger's water. (Clown 1 puts a handful of dirt in Clown 2's glass. Clown 2 stops laughing.) **Maybe that would seem only fair, but that just makes the problem worse. Now there are two glasses of dirty water.**

This situation reminds us of Romans 12:17, which says, "Do not repay anyone evil for evil." (The Narrator holds up a poster with the text printed on it.) **Repaying evil is like adding more dirt to dirty water—it solves nothing. It only makes an already bad situation worse.**

The only way to get a clean glass of water is to throw out all of the dirty water (Clown 1 pours his glass of dirty water into the bucket) and replace it with clean water (he pours a fresh glass). **That is what we are told in Romans 12:21, "Do not be overcome by evil, but overcome evil with good."** (Narrator holds up poster with the text of Romans 12:21 printed on it.) **As good overcomes and defeats evil, the clean water defeated the dirty water. Now he can have his drink of cool, clean water.** (Clown 1 pretends to take a drink.)

When someone does something bad to us, doing something bad to them in return never makes things right. Even though it is very hard to do, we can only

make things better by doing something good in return for evil. (Clown 1 offers Clown 2 the glass of clean water. Clown 2 is shocked. He takes the glass and tearfully pretends to drink from it. He pulls out a sign "I'M SORRY" and gives it to Clown 1. The two clowns then leave arm in arm.)

All for One and One for All

Theme: Church unity.

Cast: Narrator and three or more clowns.

Level: Adult.

Props: Chair, picture of Jesus, signs which list denominational nanes or names of particular local churches (e.g., METHODISTS, BAPTISTS, GRACE LUTHERAN CHURCH, FIRST PRESBYTERIAN CHURCH), signs which list parts of the body (e.g., LEG, ARM, LUNGS), and signs which read "THE BODY OF CHRIST," "THE CHURCH," "ALL FOR ONE AND ONE FOR ALL"

The Performance

Selections from 1 Corinthians can be read as desired. Clowns enter from different directions, carrying signs listing denominational names. They walk around, quite aloof from each other, and stand in separate corners.

One clown discovers a large picture of the face of Jesus on a chair at the front of the congregation. He picks it up and shows it to the congregation. He looks between the picture and the sign he is carrying, drops the sign, takes the picture in both hands, and shows the picture to each of the other clowns. All the clowns act ashamed, and drop their denominational signs.

Picking up signs listing parts of the body they act out their respective body parts. All the clowns huddle

---

*Supporting scripture: 1 Corinthians 3:1-9; 12:12-27.

together to form a "body." The picture of Jesus is held above the "body" to serve as the "body's head." Finally, the clowns hold in front of the "body" successive posters "THE BODY OF CHRIST," "THE CHURCH," "ALL FOR ONE AND ONE FOR ALL."

God's Armor

Theme: Discipleship, salvation, protection.

Cast: Narrator and two clowns.

Level: Adult.

Props: Belt, coat or vest, shoes, hat, cardboard shield, Bible, Ping-Pong balls, altar, signs ("DEVIL," "TRUTH," "RIGHTEOUSNESS," "PEACE," "GOS-PEL," "FAITH," "SALVATION," "WORD").

The Performance

Ephesians 6:10-17 is read before or during the skit. Alternately, a tape of "Soldier" by Chuck Girard, could be played.

Clown 1 enters followed closely by Clown 2. Clown 2 has the sign "DEVIL" around his neck, and he keeps shoving, poking, and laughing at Clown 1. Clown 1 staggers, falling occasionally when shoved by Clown 2, but finally reaches the altar. Clown 2 suddenly looks worried, and keeps his distance.

Clown 1 discovers, examines, and puts on a belt labeled "TRUTH," a coat or vest labeled "RIGHTEOUS-NESS," a pair of shoes labeled "PEACE" and "GOS-PEL," and a hat labeled "SALVATION." He holds a cardboard shield labeled "FAITH" and a Bible labeled "WORD." As Clown 1 puts on the armor he becomes increasingly strong and confident, while Clown 2 becomes increasingly worried.

141

After Clown 1 is fully equipped, Clown 2 throws ping-pong balls at Clown 1's shield of "FAITH," but Clown 1 is unharmed by the attack. Then, raising his Bible, Clown 1 chases Clown 2 out the exit.

Welcoming Strangers

Theme: Hospitality, judgmentalism.

Cast: Pastor and one clown.

Level: Adult.

Props: Love balloon on a stick, blackboard or overhead projector.

The Performance

This skit is done in silent mime, except for the scripture verses that are read by the "Pastor." Along with the clown, one "normal" person is needed (ideally, the pastor of the church or a stern-faced usher). The normally-dressed person pretends to be a Pastor and writes on a chalkboard or overhead projector: "TODAY'S LESSON—MATTHEW 25:42-45." While he is writing, the clown, carrying a red "Love" balloon on a stick, enters, finds a seat at the front, and sits down.

The pastor turns and sees the clown for the first time. Shocked and then outraged, the pastor walks over to the clown, points at the balloon, and shakes his head. The clown sadly takes the balloon off the stick, lets the air out of it, and ties the deflated balloon back onto the stick.

The preacher motions toward his own clothes, nodding "yes," and then motions toward the clown's outrageous clothes, shaking his head "no." The clown slowly removes his hat and several articles of his cos-

---

*Supporting scripture: Matthew 25:31-46; James 2:1-10.

tume, but the preacher still shakes his head. The clown, dragging the deflated balloon behind him, sadly leaves.

Satisfied that the strangely-dressed stranger will not disturb his Bible study, the preacher reads aloud Matthew 25:42-45.

"I was hungry and you gave me nothing to eat, I was thirsty and you gave me nothing to drink, I was a stranger and you did not invite me in (the preacher pauses)**, I needed clothes and you did not clothe me** (the preacher pauses again)**, I was sick and in prison and you did not look after me."**

They also will answer, "Lord, when did we see you hungry or thirsty or a stranger or needing clothes or sick or in prison, and did not help you?"

He will reply, "I tell you the truth, whatever you did not do for one of the least of these, you did not do for me."

The preacher looks between his Bible and the door the clown exited through. He closes his Bible, goes through the door, and returns with the clown. He gestures for the clown to sit in the front row, takes the deflated balloon, blows it up, and gives it back to the clown. The preacher gives the clown his own suit coat to wear. The preacher and the clown hug. (At this point the preacher could add a second passage, James 2:1-10, to the board and read it if desired.)

The clown walks to the blackboard, adds "HE-BREWS 13:1-2" underneath the other words, shakes hands with the preacher, gives him the Love balloon, and leaves via a different direction than his entrance.

Puzzled, the preacher looks up Hebrews 13:1-2 and reads aloud: **Keep on loving each other as brothers. Do not forget to entertain strangers, for by so doing some people have entertained angels without knowing it.**

The Deadly Tongue

Theme: Gossip, lying, swearing.

Cast: Narrator and two or more clowns.

Level: Adult.

Props: stuffed horse or hobby horse, toy boat, cigarette lighter, lasso, large bottle with skull and crossbones, drinking glass, rubber knife, play money, confetti.

The Performance

(The Narrator begins as Clown 1 enters.) **Most people don't know this, but the Bible describes the most powerful muscle in our bodies. Hey, Clown! Do you know which muscle the Bible says is the most powerful?** (Clown 1 scratches his head, and then flexes his arms in body-builder style.) **No, it's not in the arm.** (Clown 1 acts puzzled, then kicks his legs.) **No, it's not in the leg.** (He turns around, patting and flexing his back.) **No, it's not in the back.** (Baffled, Clown 1 shrugs.) **Do you give up?** (Clown 1 nods.)

The Bible says the most powerful muscle, in the body . . . is the tongue! (Clown 1 is shocked.)

The tongue may seem like a very small muscle, but listen to what James and Romans say about the power of the tongue.

We see many examples of the power of small things. We put bits into the mouths of horses to make them obey us. (Clown 1 rides a hobby horse.) **Pulling**

*Supporting scripture: Proverbs 18:20-21, James 3:3-10.

on the small bit will make the horse turn in that direction.

Or take ships, for example. (Clown 1 plays with a toy boat.) **Although they are large and driven by powerful energies, they are steered by a small rudder wherever the pilot wants to go.**

Likewise, the tongue is a small part of the body, but it makes big boasts. (Clown 2 swaggers in. He has a huge mouth painted on his face, and he pulls the corners of his mouth with his fingers to make it seem even bigger. Alternately, he might hold a large poster of a mouth.) **It can do so much damage for such a little muscle.**

Consider how a great forest can be set on fire by a small spark. (Clown 2 flicks a cigarette lighter on in front of his mouth.) **The tongue also is a fire. It corrupts and sets whole lives on fire.** (Clown 2 dances around with his lighter. Clown 1 looks worried.)

People have tamed all kinds of animals, but no one can tame the tongue. (Clown 1 tries to lasso Clown 2, but Clown 2 eludes him.) **It is a restless evil, full of poisonous lies.** (Clown 2 displays a large bottle with "LIE" and a skull and crossbones painted on it.)

Sometimes it praises our God (Clown 2 lifts his hands toward the ceiling), **and sometimes it curses people who have been made in the image of God** (Clown 2 shakes his fist angrily at Clown 1). **Blessings and cursings pour out from the same mouth. This should not be so! We would not want our kitchen faucet doing double duty as a sewer!** (Clown 1 holds up a drinking glass with tinted water, holds his nose, and shakes his head.)

The tongue also gossips. (Clown 2 whispers in someone's ear while pointing at Clown 1.) **Gossip may**

not seem as bad as lying and cursing or other fail-ures. After all, if a member of this congregation were a murderer (Clown 2 chases Clown 1 with a rubber knife) or a thief (Clown 2 catches Clown 1 and pulls play money out of Clown 1's pocket), or an atheist (Clown 2 shakes his fist at the ceiling), then everyone would be shocked. But the Bible lists gossip as a sin alongside such things as murder, fighting, greed, lying, and hatred.

The tongue kills. (Clown 2 pushes Clown 1 down and stands over him.) It kills reputations and relation-ships. It scatters lies, exaggerations, curses, and half-truths so that the damage can never be undone. (Clown 2 scatters confetti as he begins walking toward an exit.)

The tongue can do terrible things. So when we are tempted to lie, call someone names, curse, or gossip, let us keep our mouths closed and our tongues quiet. (Clown 1 runs after Clown 2, claps his hand over Clown 2's mouth, and drags him out the door.) Let us master our tongues, and not let our tongues master us.

REVELATION

Letters for Seven Churches

Theme: Spirituality, perseverance, love, communion, Valentine's Day, repentance, commitment, Christian Unity Sunday, Memorial Day.

Cast: Narrator and three or more clowns.

Level: Adult.

Props: Easel or blackboard or overhead projector, stick, giant pen, seven section signs (see text), signs ("GRACE/PEACE," "DEEDS," "PLEASURE, PRESSURE, PERSECUTION"), trumpet, white robe, menorah (seven-branched candelabra), candles, map of ancient Asia Minor, giant letters "A" and "Z," red marker, trash bag full of crumbled newspaper, red paper heart, balloon labeled "ETERNAL LIFE," halo, large magnifying glass, large cross, paper circles (small, medium, and large labeled "WORLDLY THINGS"), giant gavel, large box labeled "THE CHURCH," drinking glass, sponge, soap bar, rubber duck, soup bowl and spoon, white sheet, eyedropper, communion elements on an altar.

The Performance

We usually think of the book of Revelation as describing the future end times. The beginning of Revelation, however, consists of seven letters written to specific churches in Asia Minor, the area that is now the country of Turkey. (The Narrator places on a blackboard or easel a map of Asia Minor, with the seven cities clearly marked.) The letters were written about fifty years after Jesus died and rose again. Each letter addressed specific needs of the church to which it was written. Each letter contained both good news and bad news.

Good and bad exist in our churches today. We can learn something from these seven letters. As you watch the following drama, consider what kind of church your church is, and what kind of member you are. Those who have ears, let them hear what the spirit says to the seven churches.

(The Narrator puts on the easel or overhead projector the sign: "INTRODUCTION: JESUS REVEALS HIS WORDS")

("John" clown enters, and standing near the door, waves at the congregation.) **I, John, your brother, was on the island of Patmos, exiled there because I preached the word of God, and because I was a witness to the good news of Jesus Christ.** (A second clown enters just long enough to hit John with a stick and chase him toward the center front.) **I write this to the seven churches in the province of Asia.** (John pulls out a huge pen and pretends to write.) **Grace and peace to you from God the Father, the Holy Spirit, and Jesus Christ.** (John holds up a sign with "GRACE" and "PEACE" arranged to suggest the Trinity such as:

```
      P              P              P
      E              E              E
  G R A C E      G R A C E      G R A C E
      C              C              C
      E              E              E
```

He points to the sign and then to the congregation.)

One Sunday I had a vision. I heard a loud voice, like a trumpet blast. (Someone blows a trumpet.

151

"Jesus" clown, dressed in a white robe, enters and stands behind John.) **The voice said, "Write down everything you see and send it to the churches in the seven cities: Ephesus, Smyrna, Pergamum, Thyatira, Sardis, Philadelphia, and Laodicea."** (Jesus mimes writing and traces each of the cities' names on the map. Then Jesus places a menorah, a seven-branched candelabra, on a table or pedestal and lights the seven candles.)

I turned around to see who was speaking to me. (John turns toward Jesus.) **I saw seven candles burning. Beside the candles I saw Jesus in blinding glory. When I saw him I felt so overpowered that I fell at his feet, as if I were dead.** (John throws himself down. Jesus picks him back up.)

Then he picked me up and said, "Do not be afraid, I am the first and the last. (Jesus holds up letters "A" and "Z.") **I am the living one. I was dead** (Jesus shows the red marker spots on his palms), **and behold I am alive forever.** (Jesus mimes being buried and rising again.) **I have authority over death and the world of the dead. Write down** (Jesus hands John the pen he dropped) **what you have just seen and all that I show you.**

"See the seven candles? (Jesus points to the menorah.) **They represent the seven churches. Write the first letter to the church in Ephesus."** (Jesus points to the name on the map. If only three clowns are available, John now takes on additional church characters. Otherwise, he stands frozen in the background, pretending to write.)

(The Narrator replaces the first sign with:
"DEAR EPHESUS,
   REMEMBER, REPENT, AND RE-LOVE!
         LOVE JESUS")

These are the words of Jesus who in spirit walks among the churches and upholds their leaders. (Jesus walks around the candelabra.) **I know about all the good things that you are doing in Ephesus.** (Clown 3 enters, loaded down with a large trash bag filled with balloons or crumpled newspaper.) **You have worked very hard and been very patient. You hate evil as I do.** (Clown 4 ostentatiously enters, swaggering over to Clown 3.) **You have disciplined people for misconduct** (Clown 3 shakes a finger at Clown 4) **and driven out evil leaders** (Clown 3 hits Clown 4 with his sack and chases him out the door). **You have worked very hard, endured hardships for me** (Clown 3 carries his sack proudly), **and have not quit.**

But there is one thing wrong (Clown 3 acts shocked and drops the sack), **you have lost your first love. You don't love me as you did at first. You have become legalists and love neither me nor other people.** (Clown 3 feels his chest as if searching for something missing. He discovers and picks up a large red paper heart from the floor.) **Remember how much you once loved me! Think how far your love has fallen.** (Clown 3 glumly lifts the paper heart as high as he can, drops it, and watches it flutter down to the floor.) **Repent.** (Clown 3 drops to his knees.) **Turn back to me and love me as you did before.** (Clown 3 picks up the heart, presses it to his chest, and holds out his other arm to Jesus.) **If you don't learn to love me again, I will blow out your candle** (Jesus, standing behind the candelabra, blows out an end candle), **and you will no longer be a church.** (Clown 3 cringes.)

But those who learn to love again I will richly reward with eternal life. (Jesus relights the candle.

Jesus raises Clown 3 to his feet and gives him a balloon marked "ETERNAL LIFE.")

Those who can hear (all clowns but Jesus cup their ears attentively), **listen to the message of Jesus to the seven churches.** (Jesus motions to his mouth and then to the candles.)

(The Narrator puts up the next sign:
"DEAR SMYRNA,
FEAR NOT AND BE FAITHFUL!
LOVE, JESUS")

This message is from Jesus, who is the first and last (Jesus holds up giant letters "A" and "Z"), **who died and came back to life** (Jesus points down and then up). **I know how much you in Smyrna suffer** (Clown 4 beats Clown 3 with a stick) **and how poor you are** (Clown 3 shows his empty pockets), **but you are spiritually rich!** (Clown 3 puts his hands in a prayer position.) **I know the lies some people say about you.** (Clown 4 cups his hand to his mouth and points at Clown 3. Clown 3 trembles.) **They are evil people.** (Clown 4 grimaces.)

Fear not! (Clown 3 stops trembling.) **The devil will throw some of you in prison to test you.** (Clown 4 pushes Clown 3 down, sits on his shoulders, and puts his fingers over the other's face to simulate prison bars.) **Stay faithful even when facing death** (Clown 4 chokes Clown 3 to "death" and leaves), **and I will give you the crown of eternal life** (Jesus raises Clown 3, and puts on him a decorated cardboard crown.)

Those who can hear (all clowns but Jesus cup their ears attentively), **listen to the message of Jesus to the**

154

seven churches. (Jesus motions to his mouth and then to the candles.)

(Clown 3 removes his crown as the Narrator puts up the next sign:
"DEAR PERGAMUM AND THYATIRA,
STOP COMPROMISING WITH THE WORLD!
SINCERELY, JESUS")

These are the words of Jesus, the Son of God, whose blazing eyes see through all lies and hypocrisy (Jesus holds up a huge magnifying glass in front of his eye), **to the cities of Pergamum and Thyatira.**

I know all your deeds of love, faith, service, patience, and increasing perseverance. (Clown 3 exultantly carries with both hands a cardboard or wooden cross. Clown 4 offers him a large cardboard circle on which is printed the words "WORDLY THINGS," but Clown 3 forcefully refuses it. Clown 4 then offers a medium-sized circle with the same words as before printed. Clown 3 hesitates, but again refuses.)

But this I have against you—you have compromised with the world. (Clown 4 offers Clown 3 a small circle with the same words. Clown 3 slowly accepts the small circle. He now holds the cross in only one hand, and the circle in the other. Clown 4 gives Clown 3 the medium-sized circle then the large one. As Clown 3 accepts more circles he lowers the cross, until it is resting on the floor.)

Repent! (Startled, Clown 3 drops all his circles.) **Discipline those who are leading you into compromise, or I will discipline you.** (Clown 3 raises the cross again and chases Clown 4 out.) **I will richly reward**

those who repent of their compromise and overcome
the seductions of the world. (Jesus gives Clown 3 the
"ETERNAL LIFE" balloon and a wire halo.)

Those who can hear (all clowns but Jesus cup their
ears attentively), listen to the message of Jesus to the
seven churches. (Jesus motions to his mouth and then to
the candles.)

(Clown 3 removes the halo as the Narrator puts up
the next sign:
"TO WHOM IT MAY CONCERN IN SARDIS:
WAKE UP!
            MOST SINCERELY, JESUS")

These are the words of Jesus, the Almighty and
All-knowing one, who sees behind all surface appear-
ances. (Clown 3 stands in the middle, moving his head
and arms in a pseudo dance. Clown 4 stands directly
behind Clown 3, back-to-back, as his alter-ego. Clown 4
stands with his head lowered and his arms folded across
his chest.) You in Sardis have the reputation of being
alive, but you are spiritually dead! (Clowns rotate
together so that "dead" Clown 4 is now facing the
audience.)

Wake up! Strengthen what little remains before it
is too late! (The live clown reaches around and shakes
the dead clown awake. Then he massages and moves the
other's arms.) Your good deeds are not perfect because you have not done them with the right spirit.
Repent and obey, or I will come and take away all
that you have.

Those who can hear (all clowns but Jesus cup their
ears attentively), listen to the message of Jesus to the

seven churches. (Jesus motions to his mouth and then to the candles.)

(The Narrator puts up the next sign:
"DEAR PHILADELPHIA,
HOLD ON!
LOVE, JESUS")

These are the words of Jesus who is holy and true, the mighty and gracious judge. (Jesus holds a giant wooden gavel.) **I know your deeds in Philadelphia. I know you have little strength.** (Clown 3 crawls toward the altar.) **Yet you have kept your faith, been obedient, and have not denied me in spite of much opposition.** (Clown 4, carrying a sign "PLEASURES, PRESSURES, PERSECUTIONS," tries to keep Clown 3 from reaching the altar. As Clown 3 holds on to the altar, Clown 4 unsuccessfully tries to pull him away.)

Hold on to what you have! Hold on. You are powerless, and I will make you a pillar of the Church of God. (Jesus chases away Clown 4. Jesus lifts Clown 3 to his feet and gives him a large box labeled "THE CHURCH." Clown 3 easily holds the box above his head.)

Those who can hear (all clowns but Jesus cup their ears attentively), **listen to the message of Jesus to the seven churches.** (Jesus motions to his mouth and then to the candles.)

(The Narrator puts up the next sign:
"TO THE LUKEWARM IN LAODICEA:
BE EARNEST AND REPENT!
MOST SINCERELY, THE AMEN")

These are the words of Jesus, the faithful and true witness, the ruler of God's creation. I know your deeds in Laodicea. (Clown 3 holds up a sign "DEEDS.")

Unfortunately, you are neither cold nor hot. You are not cold like water from the refrigerator that quenches thirst (Clown 3 pretends to be drinking). You are not hot like a hot bath that relaxes tense muscles (Clown 3 pretends to take a bath with a sponge, soap bar, and rubber duck), or like hot soup that heals sick bodies. (Clown 3 pretends to eat soup from a bowl.) I wish you were one or the other! (Clown 3 drops the items.) Because you are lukewarm—neither cold nor hot—you make me sick, and I am about to spit you out of my mouth. (Jesus pretends to spit.)

You say you are rich (Clown 3 proudly displays his fine clothes), but spiritually you are poor (he pulls out his empty pockets), blind (he gropes around), and naked (he tries to cover up)! How pathetic you are! Come to me so that you can become spiritually rich (Jesus puts a wire halo on Clown 3), cover your spiritual nakedness (Jesus wraps a white sheet around Clown 3), and recover your spiritual sight. (Jesus pretends to put eyedrops into the eyes of Clown 3, who rubs his eyes and smiles.)

Those whom I love, I correct and discipline. (Jesus shakes his finger at Clown 3.) So be earnest and repent! (Clown 3 gets on his knees.)

Here I am! I stand at the door of your hearts and knock. (Jesus pretends to knock on a door.) If anyone hears me and opens the door of his heart, I will come in and eat with him, and will be friends forever. (Clown 3 pretends to open the door, he and

Jesus hug, and they go to the altar or table with a communion setting. Jesus gives Clown 3 the communion elements.)

Those who can hear (Clowns cup their ears), **we hope you have listened to what Jesus said to the seven churches.** (Jesus points to his mouth, to the seven candles, and then to all the people in the congregation. To conclude, the clowns might serve communion to the congregation, accompanied by background music.)

What Wondrous Love

Theme: Lent, love, Valentine's Day.

Cast: Narrator and two clowns.

Level: Adult.

Props: A large cross, large red paper heart, red marker, two crowns.

The Performance

(A choir sings—or tape plays—the hymn "What Wondrous Love is This" while the clowns act out this drama. All actions are performed in very slow motion.)

What wondrous love is this, O my soul, O my soul, what wondrous love is this, O my soul! What wondrous love is this that caused the Lord of bliss to bear the dreadful curse for my soul. ("Jesus" clown is dressed in a white robe. He gives Clown 2 a large red paper heart. Jesus then stands in front of the cross, lifts up his arms, and acts crucified. The audience sees red spots, previously applied with a marker, on his palms.)

When I was sinking down, sinking down, sinking down, when I was sinking down, when I was sinking down beneath God's righteous frown, Christ laid aside his crown for my soul, for my soul, for my soul, Christ laid aside his crown for my soul. (Clown 2 sinks down and sprawls before the altar. Jesus takes a fancy crown from the altar and hangs it on the cross. Jesus then helps Clown 2 stand up.)

---

*Supporting scripture: Romans 5:8-10.

To God and to the Lamb I will sing, I will sing, to God and to the Lamb I will sing, to God and to the Lamb who is the Great "I Am," while millions join the theme, I will sing, I will sing, while millions join the theme I will sing, I will sing, while millions join the theme, I will sing. (Jesus takes the crown from the cross and places it on his head. Jesus stands by the altar. Clown 2 lifts his arms toward Jesus, and then he sweeps one arm across the audience to indicate "millions.")

And when from death I'm free, I'll sing on, I'll sing on, and when from death I'm free I'll sing on, and when from death I'm free, I'll sing and joyful be, and through eternity I'll sing on, I'll sing on, and through eternity I'll sing on. (Clown 2 clutches his heart, falls down, and plays dead. Jesus walks over, touches him, and raises him to his feet. Jesus places a smaller crown on Clown 2's head. Clown 2 looks amazed, then joyfully embraces Jesus. Both clowns slowly dance out of the sanctuary. The congregation sings the last two verses of the hymn.)

The Grand Finale

Theme: Judgement, heaven, hell, future, time, New Year's.

Cast: Narrator and four or more clowns.

Level: Adult.

Props: Blackboard or flannelgraph, two large cardboard circles (one covered with foil, the other with pictures), white construction paper clouds, yellow paper sun and stars, flower, crown, trumpet, large book, a medium-sized yellow square, handkerchief, signs ("A," "Z," "DEATH," "CRYING," "PAIN"), drinking glass, spotlight or lamp, several pairs of sunglasses, "forever clock."

The Performance ▬▬▬▬▬▬▬▬▬▬

(At front center is a flannelgraph or blackboard with a large cardboard circle, representing the earth, a yellow circle for the sun, and some paper stars. The "earth" circle is covered with a collage of pictures, depicting war, famine, earthquakes, and other vignettes of suffering. The edges of the blackboard or flannelgraph are covered with white paper clouds. The "Jesus" clown, wearing a white robe, stands partially hidden behind the blackboard. The lights come on. Two or three clowns sadly and slowly carry a "dead" clown up the aisle toward the front and lay him at one side of the blackboard. The "dead" clown holds a flower on his chest.

---

*Supporting scripture: Matt. 24:29-31, 25:31-46, Mark 13:24-27, Luke 21:25-28, 1 Cor. 15:50-54, 1 Thess. 4:13-18.

The other clowns stand behind the "dead" clown, bow their heads and freeze in position. The Narrator begins.)

We often wonder about the future . . . about what happens to us after death . . . about how and when the world will end. Some people have constructed elaborate end-time schemes from scattered Bible verses. In humility, we must realize that we can not know the details of our afterlife and the world's end. But some passages of the Bible do provide a rough symbolic sketch of the Grand Finale.

The Bible says that at the end of time as we know it, there will be a great tribulation. The earth will be shaken ("Jesus" clown reaches around the blackboard and shakes the cardboard earth. The standing clowns shake and rock as if they were experiencing an earthquake.) **The sun and moon will be darkened.** (Jesus removes the paper sun.) **The stars will seem to fall from the sky.** (Jesus removes the stars and throws them on the ground.)

Then Jesus will return, coming through the clouds with great power and glory. (Jesus, wearing a crown and carrying a trumpet, majestically appears from behind the blackboard. All the "living" clowns point at Jesus. One of the "living" clowns cringes in fear, but the others rejoice.) **With a loud trumpet call, he will gather his people.** (Jesus blows a blast on his trumpet.) **Believers who have died will rise from the dead and join Jesus first, then the believers who are still alive will join him.** (The "dead" clown jumps to his feet, runs to Jesus, kneels, and hugs Jesus' legs. The standing clowns follow and do the same, except for the one cringing in fear. The fearful clown shakes but doesn't move.) **They will all be with Jesus forever.**

On that day, all the people who have ever lived

in all the centuries will be judged according to their deeds in the Book of Life. (Jesus opens a huge book, such as a pulpit Bible.) To many he will say, "Come, you who are blessed, enter the kingdom prepared for you since the creation of the world." (Jesus hugs the other clowns near him, and sweeps his arm upward.) But to those whose names are not written in the Book of Life, to those who never followed Jesus, he will say, "Depart from me, you who are cursed, into the eternal darkness and fire prepared for the Devil and his angels." (Jesus points ominously at the remaining clown, and then at a nearby door. The "evil" clown cries, cringes, and trudges to the door. The door opens and hands grab the clown. He struggles, but the hands pull him through the doorway. The door slams shut behind him.)

Jesus says, "Behold, I make all things new. I am the A and the Z, the beginning and the end. (Jesus puts a big "A" and "Z" on the board.) To all who are thirsty, I will give drink, without cost, from the spring of the water of life." (Jesus gives a clown a drinking glass. The clown pretends to drink.)

Jesus will bring a new heaven and a new earth. (Jesus removes the old "earth" circle and replaces it with the large, foil-covered circle.)

We will live in God's holy city, the New Jerusalem. (Jesus places a yellow, glitter-decorated, medium-sized square in front of the circle.) The holy city does not need the sun or moon to shine on it, for the glory of God is the light. (A spotlight is turned on Jesus, or he turns on a bright lamp. The other clowns put on sunglasses.) We will walk on golden streets. (Jesus mimes walking while pointing to the yellow square.)

God will live with us and will wipe every tear from our eyes. (Jesus again hugs each clown, and with a handkerchief wipes a tear from one of the clowns' eyes.) **There will be no more death or crying or pain because the old order of things will have passed away.** (All clowns show a different sign, such as "CRYING," "DEATH," "PAIN," "SUFFERING," then place them in a garbage bag held by Jesus. Jesus, swinging the sack in circles over his head, goes to the door, and forcibly throws the sack through the door. Jesus brushes off his hands.)

Jesus and his people will live in the new creation forever and ever. (Jesus places a third cardboard circle over the foil circle. It looks like a large clock face, but has "FOREVER" instead of "12", "PAST" instead of "3", "PRESENT" instead of "6," and "FUTURE" instead of "9." The clock's "hour" hand is pointing to "FOREVER," and the "minute" hand is pointing at "FUTURE." The clowns leave. A tape recording of "The Hallelujah Chorus," "Sing Hallelujah," or some other eschatological song is played as a conclusion.)

The Mark of the Beets

Theme: Self-parodic apocalyptic permutations.

Cast: Narrator and two or more clowns.

Level: Childish adults.

Props: Megaton nuclear warheads, a large red detonator button (do not press during rehearsals!), sign "THE END IS NEAR/HERE/THERE/REAR," portable fallout shelter, baby bib, jar of pickled beets, judgmental church member dressed in a three-piece suit.

The Performance

(One or more clowns act as parents. Another clown has a baby bib on. The Narrator begins.) **Christian parents everywhere dread the ghastly mark of the beets. Whenever parents see on their precious toddler's bib red beet juice spelling "666," they know the end of dinner is near!** (Baby clown shows the bib with a large "666" painted on it. parent clowns hold up the sign "THE END IS NEAR/HERE/THERE/REAR.")

(A knocking noise is heard. All the clowns tremble.) **Tremble they should because they know the Anti-clown is coming.** (Clowns try to hide as the door opens. A man dressed in an immaculately expensive three-piece suit enters. The Anti-clown shouts "Clowns do not belong in church! Get out!" Clowns leave slowly down the center aisle. Anti-clown offers the bib to the Narrator.)

166

The end time is here. I choose to be martyred, too rather than accept the mark of the beets. (The Narrator follows the clowns out.)

Bibliography

Clowning

DeAngelis, William. *Acting Out the Gospels: with Mimes, Puppets, and Clowns*. Mystic: Twenty-Third Publications, 1982.

Fife, Bruce, et. al. *Creative Clowning*. Colorado Springs: Piccadilly Books, 1992.

Hansen, Ruth. *The Christian Clown: A Book of Six Christian Clown Sketches in Mime*. Colorado Springs: Contemporary Drama Service, 1984.

Litherland, Janet. *Scripture Skits for a Troupe of Clowns*. Colorado Springs: Contemporary Drama Service, 1984.

Litherland, Janet. *The Clown Ministry Handbook*. Colorado Springs: Meriwether Publishing, 1982.

Roberts, Jim. *Strutter's Complete Guide to Clown Makeup*. Colorado Springs: Piccadilly Books, 1991.

Robertson, Everett. *The Ministry of Clowning*. Nashville: Broadman Press, 1983.

Sanders, Toby. *How to be a Complete Clown*. New York: Stein and Day, 1978.

Shaffer, Floyd. *If I Were a Clown.* Minneapolis: Augsburg, 1984.

Shaffer, Floyd. *Clown Ministry Skits for All Seasons.* Loveland: Group Books, 1990.

Shaffer, Floyd, and Penne Sewall. *Clown Ministry.* Loveland: Group Books, 1984.

Stucky, Mark. *The Gospel According to Clowns: Ten Skits on the Life and Teachings of Jesus.* Colorado Springs: Meriwether Publishing, 1994.

Waters, Paul H. *The Clown's Bible: A Group of Clown Sketches Interpreting the Bible.* Colorado Springs: Contemporary Drama Service, 1985.

Creativity

Benson, Dennis C. *The Bible Creative: The Gospel of John.* Loveland: Group Books, 1983.

Nadel, Laurie. *Sixth Sense: The Whole-Brain Book of Intuition, Hunches, Gut Feelings, and Their Place in Your Everyday Life.* New York: Prentice Hall Press, 1990.

Nouwen, Henri J. M. *Creative Ministry.* New York: Image Books, 1978.

O'Connor, Elizabeth. *Eighth Day of Creation: Discovering Your Gifts and Using Them.* Waco: Word Books, 1971.

Snyder, Howard A. *The Problem of Wineskins: Church Structure in a Technological Age*. Downers Grove: Inter-Varsity Press, 1975.

Sweet, Leonard I. *Quantum Spirituality: A Postmodern Apologetic*. Dayton: Whaleprints, 1991.

Von Oech, Roger. *A Whack on the Side of the Head: How You Can be More Creative*. New York: Warner Books, 1990.

Von Oech, Roger. *A Kick in the Seat of the Pants: Using Your Explorer, Artist, Judge, and Warrior to Be More Creative*. New York: Harper and Row, 1986.

Wilson, Marlene. *How to Mobilize Church Volunteers*. Minneapolis: Augsburg, 1983.

Drama and Storytelling ▬▬▬▬▬▬

Bausch, William J. *Storytelling: Imagination and Faith*. Mystic: Twenty-Third Publications, 1984.

Bennet, Gordon C. *Acting out Faith: Christian Theatre Today*. St. Louis: CBP Press, 1986.

Feldman, Christina, and Jack Kornfield, eds. *Stories of the Spirit, Stories of the Heart: Parables of the Spiritual Path from Around the World*. New York: HarperCollins Publishers, 1991.

Litherland, Janet. *Storytelling from the Bible: Make the Scripture Live for all Ages through the Art of Storytelling*. Colorado Springs: Meriwether Publishing, 1991.

Mains, David and Karen. *Tales of the Resistance*. Elgin: Davic C. Cook, 1986.

Mason, Mike. *The Mystery of the Word: Parables of Everyday Faith*. San Francisco: Harper and Row, 1988.

Owens, Virginia Stem. "Seeing Christianity in Red & Green as Well as Black & White." *Christianity Today,* 2 September 1983: 38-40.

Wright, G. Ernest. *God Who Acts: Biblical Theology as Recital*. Chicago: Henry Regnry Co., 1952.

Joy and Humor ━━━━━━━━━━━━━━

Bonham, Tal. *Humor: God's Gift*. Nashville: Broadman Press, 1988.

Buechner, Frederick. *Telling the Truth: The Gospel as Tragedy, Comedy, and Fairy Tale*. San Francisco: Harper and Row, 1977.

Cousins, Norman. *Anatomy of an Illness as Perceived by the Patient*. New York: W. W. Norton, 1979.

Cox, Harvey. *The Feast of Fools: A Theological Essay on Festivity and Fantasy*. New York: Harper and Row, 1969.

Hyers, Conrad. *And God Created Laughter: The Bible as Divine Comedy*. Atlanta: John Knox Press, 1987.

Mullen, Tom. *Seriously, Life is a Laughing Matter*. Waco: Word Books, 1978.

Mullen, Tom. *Laughing Out Loud and Other Religious Experiences*. Waco: Word Books, 1983.

Samra, Cal. *The Joyful Christ: The Healing Power of Humor*. San Francisco: Harper and Row, 1986.

Trueblood, Elton. *The Humor of Christ*. San Francisco: Harper and Row, 1964.